CodeNotes® for .NET

Edited by GREGORY BRILL

CodeNotes®
for .NET

RANDOM
HOUSE

NEW YORK

Using CodeNotes

PHILOSOPHY

The CodeNotes philosophy is that the core concepts of any technology can be presented succinctly. Building from many years of consulting and training experience, the CodeNotes series is designed to make you productive in a technology in as short a time as possible.

CodeNotes Pointers

Throughout the book, you will encounter CodeNotes Pointers: (e.g., ⌗NET010010). These pointers are links to additional content available online at the CodeNotes website. To use a CodeNotes Pointer, simply point a web browser to www.CodeNotes.com and enter the Pointer number. The website will direct you to an article or an example that provides additional information about the topic.

CodeNotes Style

The CodeNotes series follows certain style guidelines:

- Code objects and code keywords are highlighted using a special font. For example: `System.Object`.
- Code blocks, screen output, and command lines are placed in individual blocks with a special font:

```
//This is an example code block
```

WHAT YOU NEED TO KNOW BEFORE CONTINUING

The .NET Framework encompasses concepts ranging from distributed computing to database access to public key cryptography. Because the topics are so varied, the CodeNotes format is compressed and certain background information has been omitted. However, a significant number of examples and background articles can be found on the CodeNotes website (www.CodeNotes.com).

About the Authors

SHELDON FERNANDEZ is Senior Developer at Infusion Development Canada in Toronto, Ontario. He has developed software for Silicon Valley startups as well as financial and medical institutions in the United States and Canada. He has worked with Microsoft technology for many years, from his very first QuickBasic compiler to the latest suite of .NET development tools. Sheldon holds a Computer Engineering degree from the University of Waterloo and was the chief researcher on *Applying COM+*, a definitive work on Microsoft's enterprise component technology.

DEREK BARNES works as a Consultant for Infusion Development Corporation. In both Canada and the United States, he has worked on major e-commerce sites and the infrastructure for large financial institutions. His hobbies include piano, numerical analysis, and German and Chinese literature. Derek currently lives in Manhattan's Chinatown.

GREGORY BRILL is president of Infusion Development Corporation, a firm specializing in architecting global-securities-trading and analytic systems for several of the world's largest investment banks in the United States and Tokyo. He has written articles for *C++ Users Journal* and is the author of *Applying COM+*. He lives in New York City.

More information about the authors and Infusion Development Corporation can be found at www.infusiondev.com/codenotes.

Acknowledgments

First, thanks to John Gomez who saw the potential of the CodeNotes idea before anyone else and introduced me to Random House. Without John, there would be no CodeNotes. John, you are a true friend, a real visionary. I'd also like to thank Annik LaFarge, who fearlessly championed the series and whose creativity, enthusiasm, and publishing savvy has been instrumental in its creation. Thank you to Mary Bahr, our unflappable editor, who paved the way and crafted the marketing. Thank you to Ann Godoff, whose strength, decisiveness, and wisdom gave CodeNotes just the momentum it needed. And, of course, the production, sales, and business teams at Random House, with particular thanks to Howard Weill, Jean Cody, and Richard Elman.

On the Infusion Development side, thank you to Sheldon Fernandez and Derek Barnes, the writers of this CodeNote, for taking on an impossible task, in an impossible timeframe, and then turning around and delivering one of the best technical books I've ever read. Sheldon is a great writer, and Derek a great researcher—the two make an incredible team. Thank you also to the CodeNotes reviewers, who gave us invaluable feedback and suggestions on our early drafts. And thank you to the entire cast and crew of Infusion Development Corporation, who have supported and encouraged this venture throughout. I know CodeNotes was extremely trying, tough to do, and involved an awesome amount of research, writing, and editing. But here it is . . . as we envisioned it.

Gregory Brill

Contents

CodeNotes® for .NET

Chapter 1

—

AN INTRODUCTION TO THE .NET
FRAMEWORK

WHAT IS .NET?

.NET is Microsoft's new strategy for the development and deployment of software. Depending on your interests and development background, you may already have a number of preconceived notions regarding .NET. As we will see throughout this CodeNote:

- .NET fundamentally changes the way applications execute under the Windows Operating System.
- With .NET Microsoft is, in effect, abandoning its traditional stance, one which favors compiled components, and is embracing interpreted technology (similar, in many ways, to the Java paradigm).
- .NET brings about significant changes to both C++ and Visual Basic, and introduces a new language called C# (pronounced "C sharp").
- .NET is built from the ground up with the Internet in mind, embracing open Internet standards such as XML and HTTP. XML is also used throughout the framework as both a messaging instrument and for configuration files.

These are all noteworthy features of .NET, or more accurately the .NET Framework, which consists of the platform and tools needed to develop and deploy .NET applications. The .NET Framework can be distilled into the following three entities:

1. The Common Language Runtime (CLR), which is the execution environment for all programs in the .NET Framework. The CLR is similar to a Java Virtual Machine (VM) in that it interprets byte code and executes it on the fly, while simultaneously providing services such as garbage collection and exception handling. Unlike a Java VM, which is limited to the Java language, the CLR is accessible from any compiler that produces Microsoft Intermediate Language (IL) code, which is similar to Java byte code. Code that executes inside the CLR is referred to as managed code. Code that executes outside its boundaries is called unmanaged code.

2. The Runtime classes, which provide hundreds of prewritten services that clients can use. The Runtime classes are the building blocks for .NET applications. Many technologies you may have used in the past (ADO, for example) are now accessed through these Runtime classes, as are basic operations such as I/O. Traditionally, every language had its own unique supporting libraries, accessible only from that particular language. String manipulation, for example, was afforded to VB programmers via the Visual Basic runtime, whereas C++ programmers depended on libraries such as STL for similar functionality. The .NET Runtime classes remove this limitation by uniformly offering services to any compiler that targets the CLR. Those familiar with Java will find the Runtime classes analogous to the Java Class Libraries.

3. Visual Studio.NET (VS.NET), which is Microsoft's newest version of Visual Studio. VS.NET includes VB.NET, "managed" C++, and C#, all of which translate source code into IL code. VB.NET and VC.NET are the new versions of Visual Basic and Visual C++, respectively. C# is a new Microsoft language that at first glance appears to be a hybrid of C++ and Java. .NET development does not have to be limited to these languages, however. Any component or program produced by an IL-aware compiler can run within the .NET Framework. (As of this writing, other companies have announced IL compilers for Perl, Python, and COBOL.) VS.NET also comes with a fully Integrated Development Environment (IDE), which we will examine in Chapter 7. Note the VS.NET IDE now houses the development environments for both Visual C++ and Visual Basic.

OUTLINE OF THE BOOK

In this chapter we will examine the three fundamentals of the .NET Framework previously listed.

Chapter 2 provides brief installation instructions. Because .NET was still in beta release at the time of writing, these instructions may be out of date. Readers are encouraged to consult the online instructions at ⌖NET010001.

One of the goals of .NET was to eliminate the versioning problems of traditional Win32 DLLs (a problem sometimes referred to as DLL Hell). This is realized through a new type of component in the .NET Framework called the assembly, the subject of Chapter 3. .NET eradicates DLL Hell from the Windows environment by enforcing the versioning of assemblies through public key cryptography.

In Chapter 4, we will look at some of the new language features in the .NET Framework, such as attributes, which are nonprogrammatic code statements that can be used to influence application behavior, and delegates, the new type-safe callback mechanism in the managed environment. Garbage collection, a service performed by the CLR, will also be investigated, as will reflection, the ability to ascertain type information about an application at runtime.

The .NET Framework does not preclude the use of traditional COM and Win32 components that have already been developed. Mechanisms exist to allow these "unmanaged" components (those that do not run under the auspices of the CLR) to run alongside their .NET counterparts. Such mechanisms will be investigated in Chapter 5.

Chapter 6 looks at ADO.NET, the new data access model for the .NET Framework. ADO.NET is a disconnected data access model, which means that data manipulation is performed outside the context of an open database connection. This model is especially appropriate for web applications that are loosely coupled to their data sources. As its name suggests, ADO.NET is an evolution of Microsoft's ActiveX Data Object (ADO) model.

.NET also exposes new methodologies for developing standard Win32 applications. Windows Forms, the subject of Chapter 7, is the new way to construct desktop GUI applications for the Windows environment.

Internet developers will also welcome Web Forms, which brings the traditional ease and versatility of Visual Basic forms to Internet applications. Web Forms is a feature of ASP.NET, the topic of Chapter 8. ASP.NET is Microsoft's new generation Active Server Page (ASP) framework for developing robust web applications.

Chapter 9 examines Web Services and an emerging communication protocol called SOAP, which allow components to interact (i.e., transfer data, perform RPC calls) via open Internet standards such as XML and HTTP.

CORE CONCEPTS

Visual Studio.NET

Producing .NET applications and components requires a compiler that translates source code into IL code. VS.NET, Microsoft's new version of Visual Studio, contains three such compilers: VB.NET, C#, and managed C++. While a full examination of these languages is beyond the scope of a CodeNote, each language is briefly discussed below. Code examples throughout this book will demonstrate some of the nuances of each language and the syntactical differences between them.

In addition to the IDE, VS.NET contains a large assortment of command line utilities. Some of these utilities are directly incorporated into the development environment, while others are stand-alone. We will examine some of these utilities throughout this CodeNote.

Visual Basic.NET

VB.NET is the most recent version of Visual Basic, what was once thought of as VB7. VB.NET is the first version of Visual Basic to support true object-oriented inheritance, which means it has the ability to inherit and extend the interface and behavior of any class produced by an IL compiler. This is significant, as previous versions of Visual Basic could only inherit from classes written in VB itself. This feature is not really an enhancement of VB.NET but a byproduct of the language neutrality of the CLR, which gives *all* IL compilers the ability to inherit classes from one another. VB.NET also includes exception handling constructs (`try`/`catch`) similar to those found in Java and C++.

Unfortunately, VB.NET also brings about some syntax changes that will break compatibility with old VB source code. Procedure parameters, for example, are now passed by value (ByVal) by default, not by reference (ByRef). Certain syntax elements such as `GoSub`, `IsNull`, and `IsMissing` have been removed from the language altogether. For a complete list of syntax changes, see ᶜᴺ⟩NET010002. Clearly, a considerable amount of effort will be required to migrate existing Visual Basic projects to the .NET Framework.

Although not exclusive to VB.NET, most VB users will be interested in the Windows Forms (Chapter 7) portion of this book, which investigates the new way Win32 screens are developed in the .NET Framework. Windows Forms completely replaces the traditional Visual Basic

Forms editor. Finally, VB.NET now ships with a command line compiler (VBC.EXE), allowing one to write applications outside the development environment (using NOTEPAD, for example). In the first example in this chapter, we will investigate VB.NET's new compiler.

Managed C++

Managed C++ is a set of extensions added to the C++ language to allow one to produce "managed code" (code that executes under the auspices of the CLR). The most notable extension is the introduction of "managed types," which shift the burden of memory management from the C++ programmer onto the CLR. Placing the __gc extension in front of the declaration of a class, for example, allows instances of the class to be garbage collected by the CLR. This convenience comes at a cost, however, as the "managed" class must adhere to the restrictions of CLR types. It cannot, for example, inherit from two classes, even though multiple inheritance is a feature of the C++ language.

Another extension is that of managed arrays, which allows these data structures to be managed by the CLR. Managed exception handling is another amendment, differing from C++ exception handling in both syntax and behavior. Examples of managed extensions can be found at o**CN**⟩NET010003. Managed C++ is a part of Visual C++ .NET, which is the only tool in the new Visual Studio suite capable of producing unmanaged code. It is thus the only choice for producing applications that contain both managed and unmanaged code, as is discussed in the online article at o**CN**⟩NET010010.

C#

C# (pronounced "C-sharp") is a new language that Microsoft has touted as a simplified version of C and C++. In this respect, C# is very much like Java, eliminating some of the more complex features of C++ such as pointers and multiple inheritance. Most of the examples in this CodeNote are written in C# (and VB.NET), to give you a look at this new language. Like Java and C++, C# is an object-oriented (OO) language and contains expected OO features such as inheritance (the ability of a class to extend another class), polymorphism (the ability to separate an interface from its implementation), and encapsulation (the ability of objects to hide certain methods and instance variables from other objects).

Java and C++ developers will be immediately comfortable with C#, while the language may present some challenges for Visual Basic developers. Even if you choose to develop in another language under the .NET Framework, it is worthwhile to understand C#, as the majority of MSDN .NET code is written in C#. In this sense, C# can be considered the "intrinsic" language of the .NET Framework, as it was developed solely for the managed environment, as opposed to C++ and Visual Basic, which had to evolve into their .NET manifestations.

.NET and COM

While the .NET Framework is intended to simplify many of the complexities that existed with COM, it in no way renders COM obsolete. All versions of Windows today remain heavily dependent on COM, and while Microsoft's long-term vision may be to eradicate this component model, it is not going anywhere soon. Chapter 5 will investigate how .NET applications can call traditional COM components using Runtime Callable Wrappers (RCWs).

.NET and COM+

COM+ services such as transactions, object pooling, and Just-in-Time activation can be used from the .NET Framework and are accessed through the System.EnterpriseServices namespace. Examples of managed code using these services can be found at ⌖NET010004.

The .NET Runtime also implicitly uses COM+ to support some of its services. In the Transactions section of Chapter 6, we will see how the .NET Runtime automatically uses COM+ services behind the scenes to provide transactional capability for managed classes.

SIMPLE APPLICATION

In this section we look at the proverbial "Hello World" program. For the purposes of comparison, source code for all three .NET languages (VB.NET, C#, and managed C++) is given below. Readers might want to consult Chapter 2 to install the .NET Framework before proceeding.

VB.NET Application

Visual Basic developers are reminded that VB.NET now includes a command-line compiler (VBC.EXE), allowing one to develop applications outside the Visual Basic environment. In other words, you can write the following program in a text editor such as Notepad. VB users will also see from this example that VB.NET has the ability to produce console applications, something previous versions of Visual Basic were unable to do.

```
'VB.NET "Hello World" Program.


Module HelloWorld
    Sub Main
```

```
'Use the .NET Runtime Console method WriteLine,
'to output "Hello World" on the screen:
System.Console.WriteLine("Hello World!")
   End Sub
End Module
```

Listing 1.1   VB.NET Hello World program

C# Application

As with the Visual Basic example, you can write this code using any text editor. Notice that the syntax is very similar to C++ in that class definitions and methods are encapsulated within curly braces and individual lines of code end with semicolons.

```
// C# "Hello World" Program.
public class HelloWorld {
   static public void Main () {
     System.Console.WriteLine("Hello World!");
   }
}
```

Listing 1.2   C# Hello World program

Managed C++ Application

Managed C++ is almost identical to normal C++. Notice that you must use the a::b notation for namespaces, rather than the a.b notation of Visual Basic and C#.

```
// Managed C++ "Hello World" Program.
// Reference the .NET Runtime Library,
// for Console Input/Output functionality.
#using <mscorlib.dll>


void main() {
   System::Console::WriteLine("Hello World!");
}
```

Listing 1.3   Managed C++ Hello World program

Compiling and Running the Example

Assuming that these files were called Hello-World.vb, Hello-World.cs, and Hello-World.cpp, respectively, .NET console applications could be created by invoking each language's compiler from the command line as shown below (alternatively, you could create VB.NET, C#, and C++ console projects and compile them from the VS.NET IDE).

- **VB.NET:** `vbc.exe /t:exe Hello-World.vb`
- **C#:** `csc.exe /t:exe Hello-World.cs`
- Managed C++: `cl.exe /CLR Hello-World.cpp`

The /t:exe option informs both the VB.NET and C# compilers to produce executable files, while the /CLR switch instructs the Visual C++ compiler to produce IL code (this option is OFF by default).

Source Analysis
The most notable difference between the three programs is that the managed C++ example must explicitly reference the .NET Runtime classes, which is implicitly done by the VB and C# compilers. This is accomplished by inserting the following line at the top of all managed C++ programs: `#using <mscorlib.dll>`. C++ COM/ATL developers will find this command very similar to the `#import` directive used in Visual C++.

Syntactical differences aside, the three programs are remarkably similar in that they all use the Runtime `Console` method `WriteLine()` to print "Hello World" on the screen. Such uniformity is a virtue of the .NET Runtime—all three languages use a consistent set of classes to accomplish the same thing. The only difference lies in the way such classes are accessed. C++ users might recognize that we had to tell the compiler which namespace the `Console` class could be found in. The concept of namespaces and their importance to the Runtime is addressed in the .NET Runtime section of this chapter.

Topic: The Common Language Runtime

At the heart of the .NET Framework is the Common Language Runtime (CLR). In addition to acting as a virtual machine, interpreting and executing IL code on the fly, the CLR performs numerous other functions, such as type safety checking, application memory isolation, memory management, garbage collection, and crosslanguage exception handling.

THE COMMON TYPE SYSTEM

The CLR greatly simplifies crosslanguage communication through the introduction of the Common Type System (CTS). The CTS defines all of the basic types that can be used in the .NET Framework and the operations that can be performed on those types. Applications can create more complex types, but they must be built from the types defined by the CTS.

All CTS types are classes that derive from a base class called System.Object (this is true even for "primitive" types such as integer and floating point variables). This means that any object executing inside the CLR can utilize the member functions of the System.Object class. The methods of System.Object can be found at ⊶ NET010005, but for the purposes of illustration we will consider the Equals() method of this class, which can be used to test two objects for equality.

Consider the following straightforward C# fragment:

```
int a=5;
int b=5;

if (a==b) {
  System.Console.WriteLine("a is the same as b");
}
```

Since all types inherit from System.Object, the code could be rewritten as:

```
int a=5;
int b=5;

if (a.Equals(b)) {
  System.Console.WriteLine("a is the same as b");
}
```

COMMON LANGUAGE SPECIFICATION

A subsection of the CTS called the Common Language Specification (CLS) specifies how .NET languages share and extend one another's libraries. The example at the end of this chapter demonstrates how a class written in one language can be inherited and extended by a class written in another.

CODE ACCESS SECURITY

The CLR is also burdened with the responsibility of security. An integral part of the .NET Runtime is something called Code Access Security (CAS), which associates a certain amount of "trust" with code, depending on the code's origins (the local file system, intranet, Internet, etc.). The CLR is responsible for making sure that the code it executes stays within its designated security boundaries. This could include such things as reading and writing files from the user's hard drive, making registry entries, and so forth.

You can modify the permissions that are granted to code from a certain location using a utility called CASPOL.EXE. You could specify, for example, that all code originating from www.codenotes.com be granted more privileges than other code that comes from the Internet. Examples of CASPOL.EXE and an in-depth discussion of Code Access Security can be found at o⤳NET010006.

Topic: .NET Runtime Classes

In the example earlier in this chapter, all three languages used the Console.WriteLine() method to print "Hello World" to the screen. The .NET Runtime classes eliminate the need to master a different set of APIs for different languages. Instead, developers need only familiarize themselves with the appropriate Runtime classes and then call them from the language of their choice.

The .NET Runtime includes classes for many programmatic tasks, including data access, GUI design, messaging, and many more. It also acts as a wrapper around the Win32 API, eliminating the need to directly communicate with this cryptic C-style interface. The most difficult part of using the Runtime is figuring out which class you need to accomplish the task at hand. A complete list of the .NET Runtime classes can be found at o⤳NET010007.

NAMESPACES

The .NET Runtime classes are organized in hierarchical manner using namespaces. Namespaces provide a scope (or container) in which types are defined. All of the .NET Runtime classes, for example, can be found in the System namespace. In the "Hello World" example we had to inform the compiler that the Console class could be found in the System namespace by qualifying it (System.Console). Namespaces can also be nested. The System.IO namespace, for example, contains a number of classes for I/O operations, whereas the System.Collections namespace contains classes for common data structures such as arrays.

In the Hello World example we directly addressed the namespace. You will frequently see code that uses implicit namespace referencing to make it more concise. Each language uses a different keyword to include the contents of a namespace. We could have written the Hello World program in VB.NET as follows:

```
'VB.NET "Hello World" Program.
Imports System

Module HelloWorld
  Sub Main
    'Use the .NET Runtime Console method WriteLine,
    'to output "Hello World" on the screen:
    Console.WriteLine("Hello World!")
  End Sub
End Module
```

Listing 1.4   VB.NET Hello World program using namespaces

Notice that we added the Imports System line and no longer have to qualify the Console object as System.Console. In C#, you can perform the same action with the "using" keyword:

```
// C# "Hello World" Program.
// Implicit namespace referencing
using System;

public class HelloWorld {
  static public void Main () {
    Console.WriteLine("Hello World.");
  }
}
```

Listing 1.5   C# Hello World program using namespaces

As you can see, implicitly referencing namespaces can save you a lot of typing and make your code easier to read. You will use namespaces throughout the .NET framework to:

- Access the .NET Runtime classes
- Access custom classes authored by other developers
- Provide a namespace for your own classes, to avoid naming conflicts with other classes and namespaces

We will use namespaces throughout this CodeNote as we develop our own .NET components.

ASSIGNING A NAMESPACE

When you want to assign a particular class to a namespace, you use the namespace keyword. For example, the following class is assigned to the CodeNotes.HelloWorld namespace:

```
//C# hello world
namespace CodeNotes.HelloWorld
//rest of class
```

You would address any of the methods or fields of this class by using the CodeNotes.HelloWorld prefix. This naming command is identical for all three languages.

EXAMPLE

Sorting an array of numbers is something every programmer must do at some point in his or her career. C and C++ programmers have traditionally relied on the C runtime library (i.e., qsort ()) for such functionality. The universality of the .NET Runtime means that Visual Basic programmers can also enjoy the luxury of prewritten routines. The VB example below uses the .NET Runtime to sort through a list of ten random numbers. C# and C++ examples can be found at ⌖NET010008.

```
'VB.NET Example that uses the .NET collection classes
'Use the System and System.Collections namespaces
Imports System
Imports System.Collections


Module SortingExample
  Sub Main()
```

```
dim k as integer
dim oArray as ArrayList
dim oRandom as Random


oArray = new ArrayList()
oRandom = new Random()


'Add ten random numbers (0-99) to the list:
for k = 0 to 9
   oArray.Add(oRandom.Next() mod 100)
next


oArray.Sort()   'That's it!


'Print out the sorted numbers:
for k= 0 to 9
   Console.Write(oArray(k))
   Console.Write(",")
next
End Sub
end module
```

Listing 1.6   Using the .NET Runtime classes to sort numbers

Compiling and running this program produces output similar to the following:

```
10,11,61,63,74,77,80,90,94,98,
```

The bolded portions of Listing 1.6, illustrating areas where the .NET Runtime is being utilized, are worth more explanation.

```
Imports System
Imports System.Collections
```

The first two lines (above) inform Visual Basic that we will be using the System and System.Collection namespaces. Recall that namespaces are a syntactical shortcut; they save us from having to fully qualify the Runtime class names when we reference them. The following two lines instantiate the Runtime classes that we will use.

```
oArray = new ArrayList() 'no Set !
oRandom = new Random()
```

The ArrayList class is like a collection; elements can be added and removed and it will automatically resize itself. The Random class generates the random numbers that we will sort. Note that the new Visual Basic syntax does *not* require the Set keyword when instantiating classes.

```
for k = 0 to 9
  oArray.Add(oRandom.Next() mod 100)
  next
oArray.Sort()   'That's it!
```

The last code fragment adds ten random numbers to the list and sorts the array. This simply involves calling the Sort() method against the ArrayList class; the underlying operation is handled by the .NET Runtime.

As can be seen from Listing 1.6, using the .NET Runtime is simply a matter of understanding the conventions of the classes you will be calling. In the example above, the functionality of the program (sorting and output) is provided by the Runtime; Visual Basic simply acts as a forum to call it. To a large degree, your choice of .NET development language will be a function of syntactical preference, due to the universal access offered by the Runtime.

You may be wondering why we did not use Visual Basic's built-in Rnd function to generate random numbers. While we could have done this (see the How and Why section), the general practice under the .NET Framework is to use the Runtime classes where we can. In several instances, VB.NET has dropped intrinsic elements of the languages as they have been made redundant by the Runtime Classes. For details, see ⟋ₒᴺNET010009.

HOW AND WHY

Can I Still Use Intrinsic Elements (Like Rnd, Round) in My VB Programs?
To mitigate the effort required to convert existing VB projects, Microsoft has provided the Microsoft.VisualBasic.Compatibility runtime DLL, which allows you to use *some* intrinsic elements of the Visual Basic language. For examples, see ⟋ₒᴺNET010009. However, not all intrinsic elements are supported. See ⟋ₒᴺNET10009 for details.

SUMMARY

The .NET Runtime is a collection of classes that can be uniformly accessed by any language capable of producing IL code. Functionality that was traditionally provided by the language environment is now supplied by the Runtime classes. This greatly simplifies the development process, as one only has to familiarize oneself with a common framework, instead of a language-dependent API. The Runtime classes are organized using namespaces, which makes them easier to access and syntactically more concise. We will also use namespaces when we design our own components in the .NET Framework.

Chapter Summary

The .NET Framework consists of the platform and tools needed to develop and deploy .NET applications. It includes an execution environment for .NET programs (the Common Language Runtime, or CLR for short), prewritten services that programs can access from this environment (the .NET Runtime classes), and the development tools to produce such programs (VS.NET).

Unlike traditional Windows applications, .NET applications are not compiled to native machine code but are compiled to interpreted code called Microsoft Intermediate Language (IL). IL code is the inherent language of the CLR, which is similar to a Java VM, acting as an operating system on the operating system, interpreting the IL code in real time. Since IL code is interpreted, responsibilities such as memory allocation and exception handling become property of the CLR and not the programmer. For this reason, IL code is referred to as "managed" code, whereas native machine code is said to be "unmanaged."

One of the compelling reasons to develop applications in the .NET Framework is the .NET Runtime classes. Similar to the Java Class Libraries, these classes are the building blocks for writing .NET applications. Throughout this book we will use the Runtime classes for more complex operations such as database access and remote messaging. The new .NET versions of traditional technologies such as ADO are also accessed through the .NET Runtime, as we will see in Chapter 6.

Chapter 2

—

INSTALLATION

As of this writing the NET Framework is still in beta. As such, the contents of this chapter are subject to change. Please consult the online reference at ⊶ᶜᴺᵧNET020001 for up-to-date installation instructions.

SYSTEM REQUIREMENTS

In order to install the .NET Framework on your machine, Microsoft recommends the following system configuration:

- Processor: Minimum Pentium II-450Mhz (Pentium III-650Mhz recommended).
- Operating System: Windows 2000 (Server or Professional), Windows XP, or Windows NT 4.0 Server.
- Memory: 96 MB (128 MB recommended) for Windows 2000 Professional, 192MB (256 MB recommended) for Windows 2000 server.
- Hard drive: 500MB free on the drive where the OS is installed (usually C:\) and 2.5 Gigs free on the installation drive (where VS.NET will be installed).

.NET DISTRIBUTION

The .NET Framework is distributed on four CDs. The first three contain the VS.NET development tools, and the fourth contains the Windows Component Update. The Windows Component Update will install the core framework files (the CLR, Runtime classes) and updated versions of system files that the Framework requires in order to run on your machine. For information on obtaining the CDs either by mail or download, please see www.microsoft.com/net/.

INSTALLING .NET

To install the .NET Framework, run SETUP.EXE, found on the first CD. After a couple of minutes, you will be greeted with the screen in Figure 2.1.

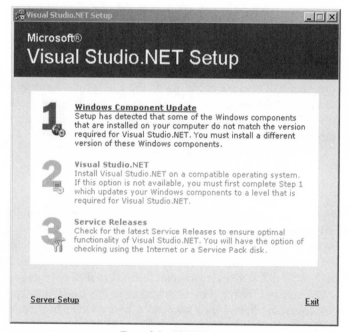

Figure 2.1   VS.NET setup

As Figure 2.1 indicates, you must run the Windows Component Update before installing VS.NET. After clicking Windows Component Update, the setup program will analyze your machine for a few minutes to determine which system files need to be updated. Depending on the operating system and the applications that you have already installed, the setup program may have to reboot the system several times during the installation process. Because of this, it offers the Automatic Log On feature.

When you supply your user ID and password, the system can automatically log on and continue the installation every time it has to reboot the machine. Because the setup program may have to reboot the machine as many as seven times during the installation routine, this option can be a real timesaver. If you disable this option, you will have to log on each time the computer reboots. (As of this writing there are some beta issues with automatic log-on, so please consult ☞NET020002 for the latest information).

After you either enable or disable Automatic Log On, the setup program will begin the Windows Component Update. Depending on the files it must update, this procedure can take several minutes. After the Windows Component Update has been completed, the setup program will prompt you for the first VS.NET CD. It will then ask you to choose which portions of VS.NET you want installed (the IDE, MSDN documentation, etc.).

After selecting those aspects of VS.NET that you want included, click Install Now. (For the purposes of working with the examples in this book, we recommend that you accept the default install options.) The setup program will begin. Depending on the options you have selected, installation will take anywhere from twenty to sixty minutes. After the installation has been completed, your computer will contain all of the necessary tools to build and deploy .NET applications.

PROGRAM LOCATIONS

The .NET setup program will append two new items to your Start menu's Program folder. The first item is called Microsoft .NET Framework SDK and contains MSDN documentation and Code samples. The second item is called Microsoft Visual Studio.NET 7.0 and contains links to the VS.NET IDE and to another folder called Visual Studio.NET Tools. We will build the majority of programs in this CodeNote from the VS.NET command line, which you can access by clicking the Visual Studio.NET Command Prompt icon shown in Figure 2.2.

Those familiar with previous versions of Visual C++ should note that you can also bring up this command prompt by running the `vcvars32.bat` file, found in the `\%Program Files%1\Microsoft Visual Studio.NET\Vc7\bin` directory.

Figure 2.2   The Visual Studio.NET Command Prompt

Finally, note that many utilities we use throughout this CodeNote (ILDASM.EXE in Chapter 1, SN.EXE in Chapter 2, etc.) are found in the `\%Program Files%\Microsoft.NET\FrameworkSDK\Bin` directory. If you use the VS.NET Command Prompt in Figure 2.2, this directory will automatically be included in your `Path` variable, so you can access the .NET Framework utilities from within any directory. However, if you use a normal Windows command prompt, you will have to manually add the tool directory to your path or provide relative paths to the tools you need to use (or run the aforementioned `vsvars32.bat` file).

Chapter 3

—

ASSEMBLIES AND METADATA

We learned in Chapter 1 that a .NET application is compiled to Intermediate Language (IL) code, which is interpreted on the fly by the Common Language Runtime (CLR) when the application is executed. It
should come as no surprise, therefore, that .NET applications must be
packaged differently than traditional Windows executables, which are
compiled directly to native machine code and immediately executed by
the Operating System.

In this chapter we cover the two fundamental aspects of component
development in the .NET Framework: Assemblies and Metadata.

CORE CONCEPTS

Common Type System

As we discovered in the Common Language Runtime section in Chapter 1, the Common Type System (CTS) defines all the basic types that
can be used in the .NET Framework and the operations that can be performed on those types. The basic type in the CTS is the System.Object
class, from which all other types are derived. This means that any object
executing inside the CLR can utilize the member functions of the
System.Object class.

Topic: Metadata

In the Runtime Classes section in Chapter 1, we saw that the .NET Runtime is a set of classes that can be uniformly accessed by .NET applications. This coherency is afforded by the CTS; because all languages are restricted to using CTS types, a level of commonality between them can be ensured.

Consider what would happen if you were to design a .NET component that used the structure depicted in Listing 3.1.

```
'In VB.NET:
public structure Age
  dim years as short
  dim days as short
end structure


// In C#:
public struct Age
{
  short years;
  short days;
}
```

Listing 3.1   The Age Structure

As a result of the CTS, all .NET clients and components will agree on the representations for a short (likewise for charts, floats, doubles, etc.). The only information a client really needs is the "type" information for the Age structure (how the Age structure is built). This information is stored as *metadata,* which is the universal format used to describe types in the .NET Framework. As we will see, metadata is used to store more than just type information. It is the format used to house security, versioning, and dependency information about components themselves. It is used by the CLR to ensure that components run against the proper resources and that they have the proper security requirements to carry out the functions they perform.

ASSEMBLIES OR COMPONENTS?

Microsoft's old Component Object Model (COM) had versioning and type information stored in both the registry and a type library (which was usually embedded as a resource in the component itself). .NET eliminates COM's awkward predicament of having component information in two locations; the metadata for a .NET component is stored entirely within the component itself. .NET components are thus fully describing in that they contain both IL code and all of the necessary information needed to execute it. This glorified type of component has been given a new physical structure in the .NET Framework, as well as a new name: the assembly.

ASSEMBLIES DEFINED

We will deal with assemblies throughout the remainder of this Code-Note, and so it is important to definitively establish what they are. An assembly is the new way executable code is packaged in the .NET Framework. What makes an assembly special is not the metadata that it contains, but simply that the CLR can interpret it in some useful manner. For example, the CLR uses metadata to:

- Ensure that an assembly's methods are called in a type-safe manner.
- Ensure that an assembly runs against the proper versions of other assemblies it depends on (the next section on Shared Assemblies illustrates this).
- Determine and provide other runtime requirements of the assembly (in the Transactions section in Chapter 6, for example, we see how one can specify that a class method execute within a transaction, which is important when database operations are being performed).

Although assemblies are still usually stored inside DLLs and EXEs, a single assembly can span multiple files (called "modules" in .NET). An assembly could, for example, span three modules. The first could contain IL code, the second resources such as bitmaps and sounds, and the third the metadata that glues them together. For this reason, an assembly is more accurately referred to as a unit of deployment, rather than a self-contained component.

WHY METADATA?

The presence of type-describing metadata in an assembly allows one to inherit a class from a compiled .NET component written in any language as if it were an intrinsic class in the target language itself. Reflect on what this means for a moment. Visual Basic developers can now inherit both the interface and behavior of classes written in managed C++. Classes written in Visual Basic can be treated as intrinsic classes in C#. Such versatility was unseen before .NET's introduction of the CLR and CTS.

EXAMPLE

To illustrate the use of metadata and assemblies, we construct a class in managed C++ that uses the Age structure in Listing 3.1. (If you don't know the C++ language, don't worry; this example is very straightforward.) The managed C++ class is then extended and used by a Visual Basic program. This source can also be found online at ⏴⏵NET030001.

```
// Managed C++ Age Class.
// Reference the .NET Runtime Library,
// for Console Input/Output functionality.
#using <mscorlib.dll>
using namespace System;


// Define the Age Structure to house
// information about a Person's Age.
__value public struct Age {
  short years;
  short days;
};


// Define the namespace that clients
// will use to reference our class:
namespace AgeExample
{
//__gc means garbage collection is on.  C++, by default, has
// no garbage collector to clean up orphaned or out of scope
// object instances.  .NET provides one, however.


__gc public class AgeCpp
{
public:
  // ToDays() takes an Age structure,
```

```
// and returns the persons Age in days.
void ToDays(Age age)
{
  unsigned long daysOld;
  daysOld = 365*age.years+age.days;
  Console::Write("C++ ToDays: ");
  Console::WriteLine(daysOld.ToString());
}
};
}
```

Listing 3.2   The Age C++ class

There are a few lines in the code that merit attention. The definition of the Age structure may raise a few eyebrows, particularly the extensions in front of the struct keyword:

```
__value public struct Age {
```

The __value extension informs the C++ compiler that the Age structure will be managed by the CLR, which is required if we wish to share the structure with other .NET components. Note that in VB.NET and C# this extension does not have to be specified, as these languages have their types implicitly managed by the CLR. Managed C++ is the only language in which such a distinction is required. We will examine the consequences of omitting the __value extension in the How and Why section later in the topic.

The public extension advises the C++ compiler that this structure should be visible to all programs that attempt to access this component. With .NET, one can specify the "visibility" of types to the outside world. The public extension is the most lenient specification, allowing access to all who want it. There are four other visibility extensions that can also be used:

* private – stipulates that a class's method can only be called directly by the class itself.
* protected – stipulates that a class's method can only be called by the class and derived classes.
* friend and protected friend – these two extensions require an understanding of concepts that we will explore in the next section of this chapter. Details on these two keywords can be found at ⟳**CN**NET030002.

The next interesting line assigns the class to the AgeExample name-space:

```
namespace AgeExample
```

The line above declares a new namespace that clients must use to access our class. Thus, to access the AgeCpp class in Listing 3.2, clients must use the AgeExample namespace, just as they would use the System name-space to access the .NET Runtime classes. The __gc extension of the next line:

```
__gc public class AgeCpp
```

informs the compiler that this type is to be garbage collected by the CLR. If you are wondering why we used the __gc extension for the class and the __value extension for the struct, it is because a struct is a value type that is not dynamically instantiated, while a class is dynamically in-stantiated and therefore requires garbage collection. A notable conse-quence of the __gc extension is that a class's destructor (if defined) will not operate in the expected C++ manner. The implications of this will be investigated in the Garbage Collection section in Chapter 4.

The rest of the C++ code is straightforward; the ToDays() method of the class accepts an Age structure and returns the individual's age in days.

COMPILATION

If the code in Listing 3.2 was named Age-cpp.cpp, an assembly could be created by invoking the Visual C++ compiler, where the /LD switch in-dicates that a DLL should be created:

```
cl.exe /CLR /LD Age-cpp.cpp.
```

Recall that the produced assembly is not an ordinary Win32 DLL; it contains self-describing metadata in addition to IL code. To look at this metadata we can use a tool provided by Microsoft called ILDASM.EXE, which allows us to inspect the makeup of a given as-sembly. COM programmers will find this utility similar to the invaluable OLEVIEW.EXE tool, which allows them to examine the internals of a COM component.

Using ILDASM

Executing "ILDASM.EXE /Adv Age-cpp.dll" at the command prompt allows us to inspect the assembly we just created and brings up something similar to Figure 3.1 below:

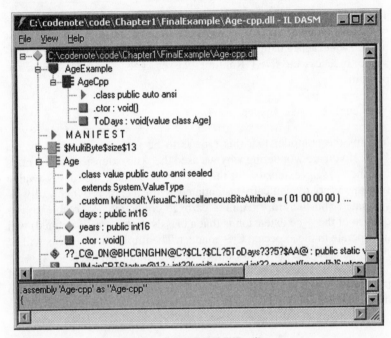

Figure 3.1   ILDASM.EXE utility

Ignoring some boilerplate insertions by the C++ compiler, you can see the makeup of both the Age structure and AgeCpp class (which is notably in the AgeExample namespace). You can also examine the metadata generated by the C++ compiler by going to View → Metadata → Show!. The metadata listing is quite verbose, but looking through it you will find the following definition:

```
TypeDef #1
----------------------------------
TypDefName: Age  (02000002)
Flags     : [Public] [AutoLayout] [ValueType] [Sealed]
            [AnsiClass]  (00000141)
Version   : 0:0:0:0
Extends   : 01000004 [TypeRef] System.ValueType
Field #1
----------------------------------
```

```
Field Name: years (04000002)
Flags     : [Public] (00000006)
DefltValue:
CallCnvntn: [FIELD]
Field type: I2
```

```
Field #2
- - - - - - - - - - - - - - - - - - - - - - - - - - - - - - - -
  Field Name: days (04000003)
  Flags     : [Public] (00000006)
  DefltValue:
  CallCnvntn: [FIELD]
  Field type: I2
```

This listing is the metadata for the Age structure that we defined, and contains all of the information that will allow other IL-Languages to use the structure. Note the [Public] specifier in the Flags section of the metadata, which means that all clients can see and use the Age structure.

Examine the metadata further and you will also find the definition for the AgeCpp class.

```
TypeDef #2
- - - - - - - - - - - - - - - - - - - - - - - - - - - - - - - -
TypDefName: AgeExample.AgeCpp  (02000003)
Flags     : [Public] [AutoLayout] [Class] [AnsiClass]
            (00000001)
Version   : 0:0:0:0
Extends   : 01000005 [TypeRef] System.Object
Method #1
- - - - - - - - - - - - - - - - - - - - - - - - - - - - - - - -
  MethodName: ToDays (06000003)
  . . .
  Argument #1:  ValueClass Age
  1 Parameters
  . . .
Method #2
- - - - - - - - - - - - - - - - - - - - - - - - - - - - - - - -
  MethodName: .ctor (06000004)
  . . .
  . . .
  ReturnType: Void
  No arguments.
```

It may surprise you to see that the AgeCpp class has two member functions when we only defined one (ToDays). You may recognize the .ctor() method as the class's constructor (VB developers can think of this as the Class_Initialize method). Note that the ToDays() method's first and only argument is the Age structure that we examined previously.

USING THE C++ CLASS IN VISUAL BASIC

As we can see, contained within the assembly is both the executable code for the class and the type information to access it. It is thus possible to inherit the class directly from the compiled assembly, as the Visual Basic program in Listing 3.3 illustrates:

```
'VB.NET Example that inherits and extends a C++ class
'Use the System and AgeExample
Imports System
Imports AgeExample


'Inherit and extend the AgeCpp class:
Class AgeVB : inherits AgeCpp
  public sub ToHours(age as Age)
    dim minutes as long
    minutes = age.years*365*24 + age.days*24
    Console.Write("VB  ToMinutes:  ")
    Console.WriteLine(minutes.ToString())
  end sub
End Class


Module Example
  Sub Main()
    dim objAge as AgeVB
    dim MyAge as Age
    objAge = new AgeVB

    'I am 20 years, 20 days old:
    MyAge.years = 20
    MyAge.days = 20
    objAge.ToDays(MyAge)      'How many Days?
    objAge.ToHours(MyAge)     'How many Hours?
```

```
        End Sub
End Module
```

Listing 3.3   Age-vb.vb – A Visual Basic program that inherits from the Age class.

We can compile the program by calling the Visual Basic compiler and referencing the C++ assembly (Age-Cpp.dll) using the /r switch.

```
vbc.exe  /r:age-cpp.dll /t:exe Age-Vb.vb
```

Run the Age-Vb.exe application that is produced, and the following output will result:

```
C++ ToDays: 73207
VB  ToHours:  175680
```

EXAMINING THE VB CLASS

Remember that Age-Vb.exe is not a standard Win32 application but an assembly packaged in executable format. As we did with the C++ assembly, we can use the ILDASM tool to examine the metadata of the Visual Basic application. Examine the metadata for Age-Vb.exe and you will find that the metadata for the AgeVB class contains the line below:

```
Extends   : 01000001 [TypeRef] AgeExample.AgeCpp
```

The metadata reflects what we expect: the AgeVB class extends the AgeCpp class. Look elsewhere in the metadata and you will find the following:

```
AssemblyRef #3
- - - - - - - - - - - - - - - - - - - - - - - - - - -
Token: 0x23000003
Public Key or Token: <null>
Name: Age-cpp
...
```

The AssemblyRef section of the metadata contains the dependency information of the assembly itself. This section of metadata allows the CLR to determine that when the Visual Basic application is executed, the Age-cpp assembly is required and should be loaded automatically.

THE MANIFEST

The section of metadata that contains the configuration and dependency information of the assembly itself is called the manifest. You can also examine the manifest by clicking on the MANIFEST icon in the ILDASM utility, as shown below.

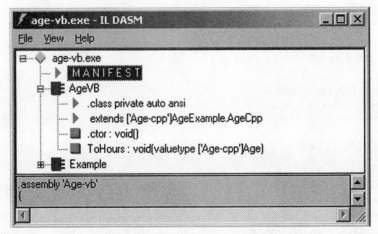

Figure 3.2   Looking at an Assembly's manifest

Clicking this icon brings up a textual representation of the manifest, shown below. Certain parts of it have been omitted for brevity.

```
.assembly extern mscorlib
.assembly extern Microsoft.VisualBasic
.assembly extern 'Age-cpp'
.assembly 'Age-vb'
.module 'Age-vb.exe'
// MVID: {7969D44A-EEC2-4609-B79B-335A9A012555}
```

As we can see, the Visual Basic application depends on three assemblies. The first is the .NET Runtime (mscorlib), the second is the Microsoft.VisualBasic assembly that provides intrinsic VB syntax elements, and the last is our C++ Assembly. Also recall that assemblies can span multiple modules. The manifest contains a list of the modules that constitute the assembly (in our case only Age-vb.dll), as well as the Module Version IDs (MVIDs) that uniquely identify them.

From this example we can see the seamless crosslanguage communication that the CLR facilitates. We wrote a class in managed C++, which was extended and used by a Visual Basic program.

HOW AND WHY

When Attempting to Run the Visual Basic Application I Get an Error Telling Me That "An exception 'System.TypeLoadException' " has occurred in C:\...\Age-vb.exe"

You must ensure that the C++ assembly is in the same directory as the Visual Basic application. This restriction occurs because the C++ assembly that we created was a *private* assembly. The CLR locates private assemblies through a process called probing, looking first in the application's directory and then in subdirectories. In the next section we will look at *shared* assemblies that can be used in a global manner.

What Would Have Happened Had We Omitted the __value/__gc Extension in Front of the Age structure/AgeCpp Class in the Managed C++ Listing?

Remember that Managed C++ is the only VS.NET development tool in which you must explicitly inform the CLR that it will be responsible for memory management of a given type. By omitting these extensions you take on such responsibility yourself, and disqualify the type from being used in the CLR. Your C++ program will compile without fail, but the Visual Basic compiler will issue an error indicating that you are trying to use an unmanaged type that it cannot access.

```
Age-vb.vb(9) : error BC30389: 'Age' is Private, and is not
accessible in this context.
```

C# and VB.NET cannot interface with unmanaged types or code directly. Instead, they must use the native invocation services examined in Chapter 5.

What Would Have Happened Had We Omitted the "namespace AgeExample" Line in the C++ Program?

Namespaces are not required under the .NET Framework. Rather, they are meant to organize your classes in a hierarchical fashion, prevent name collisions with other classes, and simplify access in general. If we had omitted the AgeExample namespace in our C++ listing, we could have also omitted referencing the namespace in our VB program and still accessed the C++ class. Namespaces are simply syntactical suggestions, but they are a convention you should follow if others will be using your components.

What Is the Relationship Between an Assembly and a Namespace?

An assembly is a unit of deployment, whereas a namespace is a scope for type definition. An assembly houses executable code, a namespace simplifies the manner in which it can be accessed. A single assembly can contain multiple namespaces. If you wrote an assembly to expose mathematical functions, for example, you might partition your code into standard and scientific services and group them into two namespaces called MyCalc.Standard and MyCalc.Scientific.

SUMMARY

Assemblies are the new file format used to house executable code in the .NET Framework. Assemblies can span multiple modules (files) and are more accurately thought of as units of deployment, as opposed to traditional components. An assembly is self-describing, as it contains information about the types it exposes and other assemblies it depends on. This self-describing information is stored in a binary format called metadata, which can be inspected using the ILDASM utility.

Topic: Shared and Private Assemblies

THE DLL HELL PROBLEM

Microsoft has touted the assembly as the end of "DLL Hell." To understand the legitimacy of this claim, we must recognize that DLL Hell came about due to the versioning problems of shared components. The idea behind the DLL was that applications could share libraries for common and useful routines. By sharing executable code, applications would be smaller, conserving hard drive space.

Problems arose with this model, because it became difficult to impose a versioning scheme for these libraries. Installation scripts would frequently and arrogantly update shared DLLs, unaware (or unconcerned) that numerous other programs depended on them. If the new shared DLL was for some reason incompatible with the old one (if functions accepted new parameters or behaved differently), many programs would cease to work.

Microsoft's Component Object Model (COM) attempted to tame

such versioning problems by declaring that a component's interface, once published, could never change. Components could evolve through new interfaces, but would never cease to be compatible with their older variants. This was a voluntary constraint, however, and developers could (and frequently would) change published interfaces, breaking compatibility with older components. Many "OLE Automation" and "ActiveX" error messages were the result of developers breaking the rules of COM.

With .NET, Microsoft has finally eradicated the problem of DLL Hell through the introduction of two types of assemblies.

PRIVATE ASSEMBLIES

Private assemblies are not designed to be shared. They are designed to be used by one application and must reside in that application's directory or subdirectory. This isolated methodology is nostalgically reminiscent of the DOS days, when applications were fully contained within their own directories and did not disturb one another. It is expected that the majority of assemblies you create will be of the private type.

SHARED ASSEMBLIES

For those special components that must be distributed, Microsoft offers the shared assembly. The shared assembly concept is centered around two principles. The first, called side-by-side execution, allows the .NET Runtime to house multiple versions of the same component on a single machine. The second, called binding, ensures that a client obtains the version of the component they expect. Together, these principles free developers from having to ensure that their components are compatible with their earlier versions. If a component evolves through versions 1.0, 1.1, and 2.0, the Runtime will maintain separate copies of each version and invoke the correct one accordingly.

SECURITY AND THE GLOBAL ASSEMBLY CACHE

What differentiates the shared assembly model from COM or Win32 DLLs is that the versioning policy is not voluntary or based on considerate programming practices but is enforced through public key cryptography. A full discussion of cryptography and its use by the .NET Runtime would quickly bring us into the world of hashing, tokens, digital signatures, and other topics beyond the scope of this CodeNote.

These subjects can quickly become overwhelming, but all you have to understand is that to enforce versioning, the Runtime must ensure:

1. that shared assemblies can only be updated by authorized parties;
2. that if a component is updated and is incompatible with its predecessor, clients expecting the older version will receive it.

These requirements are facilitated by two entities. The first is a private key that you obtain to "sign" an Assembly, allowing you (and only you) to update it. The second is the Global Assembly Cache (GAC), which can house multiple copies of a shared assembly based on your "signature" and the version information used to build it. This information (signature and version) is stored in the manifest of all clients who wish to access the assembly, allowing the CLR to load the appropriate version at runtime. Shared assemblies are best illustrated through an example such as the one below.

SHARED ASSEMBLY EXAMPLE

In this example we will consider the evolution of a fictitious assembly called WatSoft, a mathematical library for client applications. We will use C# for our example, although managed C++ and VB examples can be found at ⌒CN⋎NET030004.

WatSoft is a library that will allow clients to calculate the factorial of a number. In order to deploy a shared assembly, we must first generate a private key using the SN.EXE utility provided by the .NET SDK:

```
SN.EXE -k WatSoft.key
```

SN.EXE writes a globally unique key into the file called WatSoft. key. COM developers can think of this utility as somewhat similar to GUIDGEN.EXE, which generates unique GUIDs. Unlike with a GUID, however, we keep a private key in our sole possession and use it to sign the assembly. If someone else gained access to WatSoft.key, they could produce assemblies that looked like they were authored from us. For this reason, the private key should be guarded carefully and kept in a safe place.

Having generated a private key, we create a shared assembly from the source code in Listing 3.4 below. The code you would add to associate your application with the private key appears in bold type:

```
using System;
// the following line is needed to reference
// the two highlighted lines after
using System.Runtime.CompilerServices;


[assembly:AssemblyKeyFileAttribute("WatSoft.key")]
[assembly:AssemblyVersionAttribute("1.0.0.0")]
namespace WatSoft {
public class MathClass
{
  public uint Factorial(uint a) {
    uint nDigit, nAnswer;
    nAnswer = 1;
    for (nDigit=1; nDigit<a; nDigit++)
      nAnswer = nAnswer*nDigit;


    Console.WriteLine("Factorial v1.0.0.0");
    Console.WriteLine("{0}! = {1}",a,nAnswer);
    return nAnswer;
  }
}
}
```

Listing 3.4   The WatSoft library

The two boldface lines inform the compiler that this is version 1.0.0.0 of the assembly and that it will be signed with the key contained in WatSoft.key. These two lines are called *attributes,* which are nonprogrammatic statements that influence code generation. Attributes are covered in detail in the Attributes section in Chapter 4.

If our source file was called WatSoft.cs, we could produce an assembly by invoking C# compiler as usual:

```
csc.exe /t:library WatSoft.cs
```

The WatSoft.DLL file produced by the C# compiler can now be deployed as a shared assembly. Before we consider how a client would install and use it, a few words need to be said about the versioning scheme used by the .NET Framework.

VERSIONING AND COMPATIBILITY

The version number 1.0.0.0 is embedded into the manifest of Watsoft .DLL. Version information in the .NET Framework takes on the following form:

```
<major version>.<minor version>.<build number>.<revision>
```

The first two sections (major and minor) are referred to as the "incompatible" portions of the version number, whereas the last two (build and revision) are the "compatible" portions. When a new version of a component is released, if its major or minor number changes, it is deemed incompatible with its predecessor. If the build or revision number changes, however, it is considered compatible with its older variants. If there are two compatible versions of a component on the same machine, the default behavior of the CLR is to give a client the one with the latest build and revision numbers.

Thus, if a client is built against version 1.0.0.0 of our component and we release version 1.0.1.1, the CLR assumes the two are compatible and will give the client the component with the latest build and revision numbers, in this case v1.0.1.1. If, however, we release version 1.5.0.0, the CLR will assume they are incompatible, and clients will receive v1.0.0.0.

Keep in mind that this versioning scheme is a suggested nomenclature. The CLR has no way of ensuring that version 1.0.1.1 of our assembly is backwards-compatible with its predecessor. Since we are the only ones who possess the private key, however, we need not worry about a third party releasing an assembly that falsely claims to be compatible with ours. The private key security afforded by the CLR ensures that if we follow its versioning scheme, clients will be running compatible versions of our code.

In addition to specifying the version number of an assembly, you can optionally specify its culture, which can be used when you are deploying multilanguage assemblies. We will not use it in our example here, but consult ᐥᴺ NET030005 for details.

DEPLOYING THE ASSEMBLY

Suppose Samantha the student wishes to use v1.0.0.0 of our shared assembly. She downloads it from our website. Next, she must register it with the Global Assembly Cache (GAC) using a utility called GACUTIL.EXE. (Remember, the Global Assembly Cache houses multiple versions of the same assembly.)

```
GACUTIL.EXE /i WatSoft.DLL
```

As a result of running this utility, the file is now registered and copied into Samantha's Global Assembly Cache, which she can view by using the Windows Explorer and inspecting the \%Winroot%\assembly directory. Navigating to this area invokes the Assembly Cache Viewer, which is a shell extension that provides a friendly view of all shared assemblies on the system. (A shell extension is a component that extends some aspect of the Windows User Interface, such as the Windows Explorer.) This is shown in Figure 3.3.

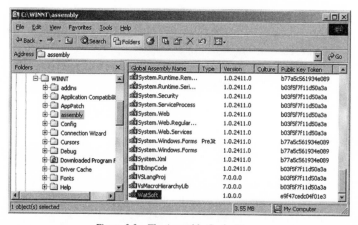

Figure 3.3   The Assembly Cache Viewer

Next to our component, we see the version number and something called the publickeytoken. The publickeytoken can be thought of as a portion of our private key that guarantees Samantha that any WatSoft.DLL updates she receives will be from us. We will revisit the publickeytoken momentarily, when we consider how the assembly is updated.

Pleased that she will no longer have to compute factorials by hand, Samantha writes the C# program in Listing 3.5, below. She also writes VB and managed C++ examples that can be found at ○^{CN}>NET030006.

```
using System;
using WatSoft;


public class MathProg {
  public static void Main() {
    MathClass mClass;
```

```
    uint result;
    mClass = new MathClass();
    result = mClass.Factorial(5);  // Should equal 120
  }
}
```

Listing 3.5   A program that uses the MathClass class

A client application is produced from the MathProg.cs listing above by referencing the WatSoft.DLL as follows:

```
CSC.EXE /r:WatSoft.DLL MathProg.cs
```

It is important to note that even though WatSoft.DLL is stored in the GAC, it must also be in the current directory so that the command line compiler can reference it.

Samantha runs the MathProg.EXE application that is produced, and is disheartened to see the following output:

```
Factorial v1.0.0.0
5! = 24
```

Unfortunately 5! (5x4x3x2x1) is 120, not 24. She alerts us of the problem, and consulting our source code we immediately recognize an elementary error that should have been caught. The line:

```
        for (nDigit=1; nDigit<a; nDigit++)
```

should be changed to:

```
        for (nDigit=1; nDigit<=a; nDigit++)
```

UPDATING THE ASSEMBLY

We promise to produce a new version of the component and e-mail it to Samantha. But how can she be confident that the component she receives is, in fact, from us? Recall from Figure 3.3 that the publickeytoken of our component is e9f47cedc04f01e3. If you use ILDASM.EXE to view MathProg.EXE's manifest you will see:

```
.assembly extern WatSoft {
.publickeytoken = (E9 F4 7C ED C0 4F 01 E3 )
```

Samantha's client application references both the assembly name (WatSoft) and the publickeytoken, which can only be produced with our private key. Together, these two entities form a "strong name," which is guaranteed to be unique. Another company could use the WatSoft namespace, but they could never generate the same publickeytoken. Similarly, Steven, Samantha's malicious classmate, cannot send her an authentic version of our component because he does not possess our private key. The publickeytoken embedded in the client application ensures Samantha that if we don't share our private key she will always call a component that is produced by us.

Having updated our source code to reflect the new change, we also modify the *AssemblyVersion* attribute to reflect the Assembly's new version.

```
[assembly:AssemblyVersionAttribute("1.0.0.1")]
```

It is important that we do NOT change the private key used to sign the component. Doing this would give the component a different publickeytoken than v1.0.0.0, and the CLR would have no way of knowing that our new assembly is an update to its predecessor.

Having received the new assembly via e-mail, Samantha installs it as she did before, using GACUTIL.EXE. If she examines the GAC's contents, she will see that there are now two versions of the component on her computer.

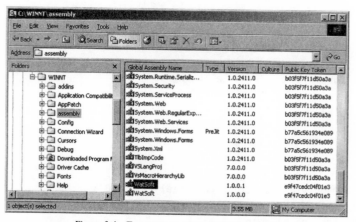

Figure 3.4   Two versions of the WatSoft assembly

Her client application does not need to be recompiled in light of the new assembly. The CLR will determine at runtime that v1.0.0.1 is backwards-compatible with v1.0.0.0 and deliver the latest of the two. The client application now outputs:

Factorial v1.0.0.1
5! = 120

Update with Broken Compatibility

A couple of months down the road, we decide that the Factorial() method is limiting because it returns an unsigned integer whose maximum value is roughly 4 billion. This may seem like a lot, but it only allows our clients to calculate factorials up to 12, because 13! > 4 billion. It would be better if it returned an unsigned long, whose maximum value is considerably larger ($\approx 1.84 \times 10^{19}$). This change breaks compatibility with the old component, however, as the Factorial() method signature is no longer the same. Realizing this, we signify to the CLR that this version of the component is not compatible with its predecessor by giving it an incompatible version number. The source for our new component is given in Listing 3.6, below:

```
using System;
using System.Runtime.CompilerServices;
// to use the 2 lines below
[assembly:AssemblyKeyFileAttribute("WatSoft.key")]
[assembly:AssemblyVersionAttribute("1.5.0.0")]


namespace WatSoft {
  public class MathClass
  {
    public ulong Factorial(ulong a) {
      ulong nDigit, nAnswer;
      nAnswer = 1;
      for (nDigit=1; nDigit<a; nDigit++)
        nAnswer = nAnswer*nDigit;


      Console.WriteLine("Factorial v1.0.0.0");
      Console.WriteLine("{0}! = {1}",a,nAnswer);
      return nAnswer;
    }
  }
}
```

Listing 3.6   A new version of the WatSoft library

Even if Samantha installs this version of the component on her computer, the CLR will direct her client to version 1.0.0.1 of the component.

Because of the Runtime's versioning semantics, new clients can take advantage of the new component while existing clients continue to rely on an older, compatible one.

If Samantha wanted to take advantage of the new method, she would modify her code (Listing 3.5) by changing the result variable from a uint to a ulong, and then recompile her application against the new assembly. Her client application will now reference v1.5.0.0 of the assembly, which will allow her to compute significantly larger factorials.

Some of you may be wondering where exactly the various versions of Watsoft.DLL reside on Samantha's machine (where exactly is the GAC?). As of this writing, versions 1.0.0.0, 1.0.0.1, and 1.5.0.0 of the component with the aforementioned publickeytoken can be found in the following directories (they are copied there by GACUTIL.EXE):

```
\%winroot%\Assembly\GAC\WatSoft\1.0.0.0__e9f47cedc04f01e3\
WatSoft.DLL
\%winroot%\Assembly\GAC\WatSoft\1.0.0.1__e9f47cedc04f01e3\
WatSoft.DLL
\%winroot%\Assembly\GAC\WatSoft\1.5.0.0__e9f47cedc04f01e3\
WatSoft.DLL
```

As can be seen, each version of the component is stored in a directory that is based on its version number and publickeytoken. This is designed to avoid name clashes. If another company released an assembly also called WatSoft.DLL, it would reside in a different directory because its publickeytoken would be different. Not surprisingly, the GAC's directories can only be modified by someone with administrator privileges.

BACK TO PRIVATE ASSEMBLIES

In light of our knowledge of shared assemblies, we can say a few things about their private counterparts. Unlike shared assemblies, private assemblies are not signed with a key and thus do not have strong names. This is permissible, because they are only to be used by one application, so unique naming is not a concern. Private assemblies also cannot be registered in the GAC using GACUTIL.EXE. Futhermore, no version checking is performed on private assemblies. While it is possible to embed a version number into a private assembly using the AssemblyVersion attribute we used in Listing 3.6, it is effectively ignored by the Runtime.

Finally, recall that the client application's manifest contained the version and publickeytoken of the WatSoft shared assembly. This allows the CLR to load the proper version and ensure that the assembly was authored by us. The publickeytoken also allows the CLR to determine that the assembly's contents (IL-code, resources, etc.) have not been corrupted or tampered with. The CLR not only assures Samantha that she is running our code, it also assures her that the integrity of the assembly has not been compromised since we signed it.

Likewise, if WatSoft.DLL uses an assembly itself, the CLR would ensure that it ran against the proper version. These integrity checks are performed throughout the chain of callers. Samantha is guaranteed not only that she is calling our code, but that our code is calling who it expects, and so on. One can see that the versioning provided by the CLR is truly rigorous.

HOW AND WHY

Can I Change the Runtime's Versioning Rules?

In some situations it may be desirable to change how the Runtime determines the version of a component that is loaded. In our example, we may wish for clients built on v1.0.0.0 of the WatSoft component to use v1.5.0.0 if it is available, even though the semantics stipulate that the version numbers are incompatible. We can accomplish this by using XML configuration files to override the default versioning behavior of the Runtime. An application configuration file can override the versioning rules for the application, while an administrator configuration file can override the policy for the entire machine. Details on using both of these file types can be found at ᵒᶜᴺᵞNET030007.

Are Assemblies with Strong Names Trustworthy?

While a strong name can assure you that an assembly comes from the person who originally authored the component, it makes no guarantees about who that person is. Anyone can generate a private key using SN.EXE and distribute a shared assembly, claiming it originates from company XXX. Identity is only guaranteed through Microsoft's Authenticode technology, information on which can be found at ᵒᶜᴺᵞNET030008.

Do Shared Assemblies Have to Have Version Numbers?

If you do not specify a version number when creating a shared assembly (i.e., if we had omitted the AssemblyVersion attribute in Listing 3.5), then the compiler will automatically give your component a version number of 0.0.0.0. Clients will be bound to this version number with the normal versioning rules.

Do I Have to Use Attributes to Specify the Key Location and Version Number?

In our example we used the `AssemblyKeyFile` and `AssemblyVersion` attributes to specify the private key file and component version number. Alternatively, you can use a .NET utility called AL.EXE to specify this information at compile time. This is a more involved process, however, and results in an assembly that consists of two modules, one for your IL code and one that contains the manifest with signature information. An example that uses AL.EXE to build the WatSoft shared assembly can be found at ⌐ᴺ⟩NET030009.

Do Assemblies with Strong Names Have to Be Registered in the GAC?

If you give an assembly a strong name by signing it with a private key, you only have to register it with the GAC if you want it to be shared. If it is not registered with the GAC, a strong-named assembly will function much like a private one, being accessible only to applications within its directory. The advantage of this approach is that these strong private assemblies will be more secure than normal private ones, because the CLR will still perform version and signature checking on them.

SUMMARY

Shared assemblies solve the problem of DLL Hell through the Global Assembly Cache (GAC), which allows multiple versions of an assembly to exist side-by-side on the same machine, and through public key cryptography, which ensures that an assembly can only be updated by an authorized party. To create a shared assembly you must sign it using a private key (obtained through the SN.EXE utility) and give it a version number using the CLR's prescribed semantics. The version number allows you to specify whether or not an assembly is backwards-compatible with its predecessor, which allows the CLR to perform Runtime version checking. The CLR also verifies the integrity of shared assemblies, ensuring that their contents (IL code, resources, etc.) have not been compromised since they were created.

Private assemblies don't really solve the DLL Hell problem so much as avoid it. They are intended to be called by one application and must reside in that application's directory or subdirectory. Because private assemblies don't reside in a prescribed shared area, there is less chance of these assemblies falling prey to malicious (or negligent) installation scripts that wish to update them. Unlike shared assemblies, private ones are not afforded the luxury of version and signature checking.

Chapter Summary

Components and executables are now packaged differently in the .NET Framework and have matured into assemblies. Assemblies contain both IL code and metadata. Metadata describes the types an assembly exposes, the assembly's dependencies, and security and versioning information of the assembly itself. The CLR uses an assembly's metadata to ensure that its methods are called in a type-safe manner and that an assembly runs against its proper resources.

The .NET Framework eradicates the DLL Hell problem through the shared assembly, which must reside in the Global Assembly Cache (GAC). A shared assembly must be signed with a private key (generated with the SN.EXE utility), which allows only authorized parties to update the assembly as it evolves. The GAC is capable of storing multiple versions of the same assembly on one system, while the CLR's versioning rules ensure that clients receive compatible versions of assemblies they were built against. The CLR's enforcement of versioning through public key cryptography is considerably stronger than older shared-component models such as Win32 DLLs and COM, where cooperative versioning is dependent on considerate programming practices and voluntary rules.

Chapter 4

—

.NET LANGUAGE FEATURES

In this chapter we examine some of the language features in the .NET Framework. These are not really language-specific features, but rather services provided by the language-neutral CLR. As such, the services discussed in this chapter are available to any program written in C#, VB.NET, or managed C++.

The first two topics, Attributes and Reflection, are centered around an assembly's metadata. As you will recall, metadata makes an assembly self-describing, and assists the CLR in ensuring that clients call methods in a type-safe manner. Reflection extends the benefits of metadata by allowing developers to inspect and use it at runtime. Using reflection one could, for example, dynamically, determine all the classes contained in a given assembly and invoke their methods, if desired.

Attributes are declarative tags in code that insert additional metadata into an assembly, where it can be consumed by the CLR, or possibly yourself, to influence some aspect of your application (how it behaves, how it is deployed, etc.).

The last two topics in this chapter, Delegates and Garbage Collection, provide type safety for callback functions and automatic memory management, respectively. C++ programmers can think of delegates as glorified callback functions, whereas Visual Basic developers should know that delegates are the mechanism behind VB.NET's Event model. Delegates facilitate "multicasting," which is equivalent to a single source calling several function pointers or raising multiple events.

Garbage collection, a service afforded to any application running within the CLR, destroys objects once they are no longer being referenced. Although garbage collection may sound like an innocuous operation, we shall see that is has important implications as to how objects must release their resources.

CORE CONCEPTS

An AppDomain is the protection boundary for code executing in the .NET Framework. Conceptually, you can think of it as the .NET equivalent of a Win32 process. If IL code misbehaves, the CLR shuts down the AppDomain, much as the Windows Operating System shuts down a process that has executed illegal native code. And just as a process can load multiple DLLs, an AppDomain can house multiple assemblies. This information will be important when we consider the process of reflection and begin probing .NET entities to determine the types they contain.

Although conceptually similar, an AppDomain and a Win32 process are different from a Windows architecture perspective. Win32 processes must provide robust protection against native code, making them expensive to create and tear down. Because IL code operates inside the CLR, it can be afforded the same protection without the costly construction of a process. The .NET Framework saves resources by allowing multiple AppDomains to exist in one process. If the CLR must shut down an AppDomain, it can do so without disrupting other AppDomains in the same process. It is proper, therefore, to think of an AppDomain as a lightweight process, made possible by the increased protection provided by the CLR.

The relationship between AppDomains and Win32 processes will be revisited in Chapter 5, when we investigate how to call native code from the .NET environment.

Topic: Attributes

Attributes are nonprogrammatic statements that embed additional metadata into an assembly. This metadata can then be extracted at runtime to characterize aspects of an application or to influence its behavior. In the section on private and shared assemblies in Chapter 3, for example, we saw how the AssemblyVersion attribute was used to specify an assembly's version number:

The following line in C#

```
[assembly:AssemblyVersionAttribute("1.0.0.0")]
```

caused the C# compiler to embed the following metadata into the generated assembly:

```
.assembly WatSoft as "WatSoft"
{
  ... // other metadata
  .ver 1:0:0:0
}
```

When an application uses the assembly, the CLR extracts this section of the metadata to determine if the versioning requirements of the application have been met.

Attributes are used throughout the .NET Framework. The CLR uses them to determine how objects are serialized, whether or not an object will be utilizing COM+ services such as transactions, and so on. The CLR is not the only consumer of attribute-generated metadata, however. The Windows Forms designer that we will examine in Chapter 7, for example, uses attributes extensively to determine how controls are displayed.

There exist two types of attributes in the .NET Framework: *predefined* attributes such as AssemblyVersion, which already exist and are accessed through the Runtime Classes; and *custom* attributes, which you write yourself by extending the System.Attribute class. We will explore custom attributes in the next section on Reflection, once we have a better feel for how attributes work. To this end, we will now explore the predefined Conditional attribute, which is a new way of writing conditional compilation statements in the .NET Framework.

EXAMPLE

For years, developers have relied on conditional compilation techniques to reduce the size of their applications and to debug their programs. A C++ program, for example, might #define a DBG directive to turn trace messages on and off:

```
#define DBG
...
#ifdef DBG
```

```
Console::WriteLine("[TRACE]: In Function . . . ");
#endif
```

A Visual Basic program would accomplish the same thing by using the #CONST statement:

```
#Const DBG = True
...
#If DBG = True Then
  Console.WriteLine("[TRACE]: In Function . . .");
#End If
```

In the .NET Framework, you can also use the Conditional attribute found in the System.Diagnostic namespace to facilitate conditional compilation. This may not seem terribly exciting, until you realize that the Conditional attribute allows an assembly to determine how its *client* will compile, depending on the directives defined in the client. The following VB example will clarify this. C# and managed C++ examples can be found at ⌁NET040001.

```
Imports System
Imports System.Diagnostics

namespace condExample
  public class condClass
    'Apply the Conditional attribute to MyFunction:
    <ConditionalAttribute("DBG")> public shared sub
      MyFunction
        Console.WriteLine("DBG directive is defined...")
      end sub
  end class
end namespace
```

Listing 4.1   condClass.vb

First, note that in Visual Basic attributes are defined with the syntax <MyAttribute>, as opposed C#'s syntax [MyAttribute]. Also note that nothing in this assembly is conditionally compiled. Rather, the Conditional attribute poses the following question to all compilers that are compiling applications that reference this assembly:

Does the application you are compiling have DBG defined?
  • YES: I'll allow your client to call MyFunction(), compile your application as if it called the method.

- NO: Your client cannot call `MyFunction()`, compile your application as if it never called the method.

This information is communicated via the assembly's metadata, which, if you inspect it using the ILDASM tool, resembles the following text (don't forget to create the assembly using the VB compiler: `vbc.exe /t:library condClass.vb`):

```
MethodName: MyFunction (06000001)
    . . .
    System.Diagnostics.ConditionalAttribute . . .
    . . .
    ctor args: ("DBG")
```

Keeping this metadata in mind for a moment, consider the following C# client that uses the assembly:

```
using System;
using condExample;

public class MyClass {
  public static void Main() {
    condClass.MyFunction();
  }
}
```

Listing 4.2   condClassClient.cs

When we compile this application as follows:

```
csc.exe /r:condClass.dll condClassClient.cs
```

the C# compiler asks itself the question implied by `Conditional` attribute to determine whether `MyFunction()` is called or not. In this case, there is no DBG defined in the client application, and so `MyFunction()` is not called (it would be as if the line were never in the source code in the first place). If however, you were to add the following line to the top of the listing:

```
#define DBG
```

`MyFunction()` would be called, resulting in the following output:

```
DBG directive is defined...
```

You can confirm that the presence of the #define DBG statement toggles, whether or not the function is being called, by using ILDASM to examine the application's IL code under both scenarios.

This example illustrates yet another language-neutral aspect of the .NET environment: compilation directives can be shared among any compiler that targets the CLR. This is just one example of using attributes, but it highlights the underlying premises behind them:

- That an attribute embeds additional metadata into the assembly.
- That metadata is used in some fashion to influence application behavior.

By convention, the names of all of the predefined attributes found in the Runtime classes end with "Attribute" (e.g., AssemblyVersionAttribute, ConditionalAttribute, etc.). To make your code less verbose, C#, VB.NET, and managed C++ allow you to refer to attributes without specifying this redundant ending. Thus, in our previous example we could have referenced ConditionalAttribute simply as Conditional, a convention we will follow throughout the remainder of this CodeNote.

HOW AND WHY

Why Do I Get the Following Error When I Use the Conditional Attribute: "CS0578: Conditional not valid on "MyFunction()" because its return type is not void"?
The Conditional attribute can only be used on functions without return values. Consider what would happen if a client had the following line of code:

```
result = someConditionalFunction();
```

Remember that the Conditional attribute stipulates that if the client doesn't have a certain directive defined, the client is compiled as if the call to the function had never proceeded. If this occurs, what will the value of result be? Other portions of the client depending on result to contain a valid value will be thwarted. Because of the problems associated with this scenario, the Conditional attribute can be used only on functions without return values.

SUMMARY

There are two types of attributes in the .NET Framework, both of which embed additional metadata into an assembly. Predefined attributes are accessed through the Runtime classes, and the metadata they produce is used by some Microsoft entity (such as the CLR or Windows Form Designer) for descriptive purposes or to influence application behavior. Custom attributes allow developers to place their own metadata into assemblies, which can be retrieved using the reflection technique examined in the next topic.

Topic: Reflection

Metadata is the language that glues the .NET Framework together. In Chapter 3, we saw that assemblies use metadata to describe the types they contain, so that applications can effectively communicate with them. In the previous section, we saw that predefined attributes embed additional metadata into an assembly, which, in turn, is used by some entity in the .NET Framework (such as the CLR or the Windows Form Designer) for informational purposes or to affect application behavior.

The virtue of self-describing metadata becomes most apparent when we consider the process of reflection, which allows a developer to probe and use an assembly's metadata directly. You can, for example, determine all the classes that an assembly contains, the members exposed by the classes, and the parameters the members expect, all without prior knowledge of the assembly. Using this information, you can call a class's method dynamically by constructing its parameters at runtime. COM developers will find this analogous to late binding, which allows you to call a component's methods without a prior knowledge of its makeup.

From an external point of view, an assembly is simply a collection of exposed types. These types could be the basic types found in the Common Type System (CTS) such as integers and strings, or more complex constructions of those types, such as classes, structures, and enumerations. Recalling that an AppDomain can contain multiple assemblies and that an assembly can contain multiple modules, we can construct the following hierarchy of elements within the .NET Framework:

AppDomains:
  Assemblies:
    Modules:
      Types:

Fields
Properties
Events
Methods
Other Types

The classes found in the System.Reflection namespace allow you to probe through an assembly's metadata in a similar hierarchical fashion. You can, for example, ascertain all the types contained within an assembly (its classes, structures, etc.). Similarly, given a class, you could determine the types it contains (the class's methods and member variables) as well as their constituent types (method parameters and return values). Class inspection using reflection is demonstrated in the upcoming example.

Reflection can also be used to retrieve the metadata that has been embedded as a result of an attribute. This is especially important for custom attributes, whose metadata you will want to retrieve and use in some meaningful way. The second example in this section will demonstrate this tactic.

Just as reflection can be used to retrieve and interpret metadata, it can be used to construct and "emit" it. The classes found in the System.Reflection.Emit namespace allow metadata for new types to be generated in memory and used at runtime. In fact, you can dynamically create an entire assembly, its classes and methods, and the IL code behind them. The "in memory" assembly can then be used by other applications. Examples of this versatile procedure can be found at ⚬**CN**⟩NET040002.

BASIC REFLECTION

In this example we will consider how reflection can be used to probe and call a mathematical library called WatSoft, written in C#. For the sake of brevity, the method implementations have been omitted; however, full versions of C#, VB, and managed C++ source code can be found at ⚬**CN**⟩NET040003.

```
namespace WatSoft {
public class MathClass {
  public string SomeVar;
  public ulong Factorial(ulong a) {
    // Implementation Omitted
  }
  private int Add(int a, int b) {
```

```
    // Implementation Omitted
  }
}
}
```

Listing 4.3   WatSoft.cs

As usual, we would create a WatSoft DLL assembly using the C# compiler:

```
csc.exe /t:library WatSoft.cs
```

We know that the WatSoft.DLL file produced contains the metadata needed to describe MathClass's members: the public member variable SomeVar; and the public and private methods, Factorial() and Add(). A client program can probe this metadata using the System.Reflection classes, as the following C# program demonstrates. VB and Managed C++ examples can be found at ⌐ℕ⌐NET040004.

```
// Remember to run the compiler with /r:Watsoft.dll
using System;
using System.Reflection;
using WatSoft;

public class Reflect  {
public static void Main() {
  MathClass MyClass;
  MyClass = new MathClass();

  // Print out the member information of Mathclass:
  Type T = MyClass.GetType();
  MemberInfo[] Members =
    T.GetMembers(BindingFlags.LookupAll);
  foreach (MemberInfo mi in Members)
    Console.WriteLine(" {0} = {1}", mi.MemberType,mi);
}
}
```

Listing 4.4   WatDepict.cs

Running this program will print out all the members of MathClass (note the inherited methods of System.Object, such as GetHashCode).

```
Field = System.String PublicMemberVar
Method = Void Finalize()
```

```
Method = Int32 GetHashCode()
Method = Boolean Equals(System.Object)
Method = System.String ToString()
Method = UInt64 Factorial(Uint64)
Method = Int32 Add(Int32, Int32)
Method = System.Type GetType()
Method = System.Object MemberwiseClone()
Constructor = Void .ctor()
```

The key to understanding the process of reflection is to familiarize yourself with its underlying classes. An object's metadata is accessed through its Type class, which is retrieved using its GetType() method. GetType() is implemented by the System.Object class from which all classes derive, so it can be called on any object:

```
Type T = MyClass.GetType();
```

MyClass's metadata can now be accessed through the Type class. One of the members of the Type class is GetMembers(), which returns the members of the underlying object as an array of MemberInfo objects:

```
MemberInfo[] Members =   T.GetMembers(BindingFlags.Instance|
BindingFlags.NonPublic|BindingFlags.Public);
```

GetMembers() can accept an optional parameter that specifies the members it will return. In this case, we have requested that it return *all* members (private, public, and constructor) by using the combination of BindingFlag members found in the System.Reflection namespace. Had we omitted this parameter and simply written:

```
MemberInfo[] Members = T.GetMembers();
```

GetMembers() would have only returned public methods (the default setting).

Having executed this method, we are now left with an array of MemberInfo objects, each of which represents a member of the Math-Class class. We iterate through each element in the array and print its information:

```
foreach (MemberInfo mi in Members)
  Console.WriteLine(" {0} = {1}", mi.MemberType,mi);
```

Visual Basic developers should be familiar with the for each construct, which provides a straightforward way to iterate through arrays and collections. As can be seen from the code above, this feature is also available in C#.

The System.Reflection classes provide access to the wealth of information embedded in an assembly's metadata. You can retrieve and use all of this data by using the appropriate combination of System .Reflection classes. For some additional examples that use reflection to probe metadata, see ℴ𝐂𝐍NET040005.

ADVANCED REFLECTION

The basic reflection example may not seem particularly impressive, as it doesn't yield any information that we probably don't already know. After all, if we have access to WatSoft.DLL, then we can inspect the MathClass's methods using the ILDASM tool instead of using reflection to interpret the metadata ourselves.

The true versatility of reflection becomes apparent when you consider the following C# program, which calls the WatSoft assembly without any prior knowledge of its makeup. VB and managed C++ examples can be found at ℴ𝐂𝐍NET040006.

```
public class Reflect {
public static void Main()  {
  // Dynamically load the assembly:
  Assembly asm = Assembly.LoadFrom("WatSoft.dll");

  // Iterate through the Assembly, and search
  // all its classes for a method named "Add"
  // that takes two Int32s as parameters:
  foreach (Type T in asm.GetTypes()) {
    Console.WriteLine("Searching Class: {0} for an" +
      "Add() method",t);
    MethodInfo[] miarr =
      t.GetMethods(BindingFlags.Instance|
      BindingFlags.NonPublic| BindingFlags.Public);
    foreach (MethodInfo mi in miarr) {
      if (mi.Name == "Add") {
        ParameterInfo[] pInfo  = mi.GetParameters();

        // Does this Add() take two int32 parameters?
```

```
        if (pInfo.Length == 2) {
          if (pInfo[0].ParameterType.Equals(typeof(Int32)) &&
             pInfo[1].ParameterType.Equals(typeof(Int32)))
          {
            Console.WriteLine("Add() found with two " +
              "Int32 parameters.");

            // Create an instance of the class:
            object o = Activator.CreateInstance(t);

            // Construct the parameters required to call
            // the call the Add method using Invoke():
            Object returnValue;
            Object [] arguments = new Object[2];
            arguments[0] = 1;
            arguments[1] = 2;

            // Dynamically Invoke Add():
            returnValue = mi.Invoke(o,arguments);
            Console.WriteLine("Dynamically Invoked " +
              "Add(1,2) = {0}",returnValue);
          }
        }
      }
    }
  }
}}
```

Listing 4.5   WatCall.cs: dynamically calling MathClass.Add( )

This program works in a fashion similar to that of the basic reflection example, using the classes found in `System.Reflection` to probe the various types in the assembly. The difference is that the assembly is loaded dynamically at runtime using the `Assembly` class's `LoadFrom()` method, instead of being linked at compile time. Every class in the assembly is then searched for an `Add()` method that accepts two integer parameters. When such a method is found, it is called using the `Invoke()` method of the `MethodInfo` class:

```
Object returnValue;
Object [] arguments = new Object[2];
arguments[0] = 1; arguments[1] = 2;
returnValue = mi.Invoke(o,arguments);
```

As the code above illustrates, parameters are passed to the `Invoke()` method as an array of `objects`, with the first element corresponding to the first parameter and so on. It is up to us to ensure that we deliver an object array whose size and contents match the parameters and types that the method is expecting. If we fail to do this, the CLR will throw a `TargetParameter` or `Argument` exception.

Note that this example, unlike the previous program, does not require compilation with the /r:WatSoft.DLL switch. Everything from loading the assembly to calling its method is done dynamically at runtime. However, Watsoft.DLL must reside within the same directory as the application program, because the DLL was identified without a path (`LoadFrom("Watsoft.DLL")`). If the DLL were contained in another directory, we would have used a qualified name, such as `Assembly .LoadFrom("\SomeOtherDir\WatSoft.dll")`.

Running this program produces the following output:

```
Searching Class: WatSoft.MathClass for an Add() method
Found a method called Add with two Int32 parameters.
Dynamically Invoked Add(1,2) = 3
```

Look carefully and you'll realize that we have done something that we shouldn't have been able to do: `Add()` is a private method in MathClass (see Listing 4.3). In addition to dynamic-invocation services, reflection has the dubious benefit of allowing you to invoke private methods on classes. This can be useful for diagnostic utilities that need to interact with classes beyond their public interfaces, but it raises security concerns for class authors who thought their private methods would be, well, private. Whether or not code can invoke private methods using reflection depends on the security policy wherever the code originates (locally, the Internet, etc.). By default, code that originates from the local hard drive can detect and invoke the private methods of a class. You can alter this behavior by changing the security policy for the entire machine using a utility called CASPOL.EXE. Details on how to do this can be found at CN NET040007.

Programmers familiar with COM would be right in thinking that the code in Listing 4.5 is very similar to calling a COM component through COM's late-binding mechanism (`IDispatch` if you are a C++ programmer, or the `Object` type if you are familiar with Visual Basic). Not only is the syntax very similar, but the premise is as well. Dynamic invocation through both reflection and late-binding can be used when a developer has no prior knowledge of the assembly. They can be used to determine if a class (interface in COM) implements a certain method, and to invoke it if desired. Unlike ordinary late-binding, however, you can use reflection to determine whether an object supports a given method before trying to call it and receiving the corresponding result or "Method Not Found" error.

CUSTOM ATTRIBUTES

In the previous example, the metadata in WatSoft.DLL allowed us to dynamically call the Add() method using reflection. This metadata was of the standard variety—it was produced by the C# compiler to describe all the types contained within the assembly. Attributes also produce metadata that we can exploit through reflection.

Up to this point, we have differentiated between predefined attributes, which already exist, and custom attributes, which you write yourself. The reality is that all attributes *are* custom attributes, the only difference being that predefined ones have already been written and packaged by Microsoft. (There is one caveat to this generalization, which we will examine momentarily.) To design a custom attribute, you must write a class that inherits from the System.Attribute class. The arguments of the class's constructor define the parameters of the attribute. If, for example, the class's constructor accepts a single string argument, then the attribute, when used by a client, must be declared with a single string (the Conditional attribute in Listing 4.1 is an example of an attribute that accepts a single string).

To distribute your custom attribute you compile the class into an assembly. Clients that reference the assembly, however, do not use the class as they normally would (instantiating it, calling its methods, etc.). Instead, they use the class like . . . an attribute, as a nonprogrammatic statement with the proper parameters:

```
[SomeCustomAttribute(a=4,b=5)]
```

The important point to note is that an attribute's parameter values (4 and 5 in the line above) get embedded as metadata into the client's assembly. When the client's assembly is loaded, the CLR retrieves these parameters and delivers them to your class, where it can do something useful with them. The upcoming example will clarify this.

Another important point to note is that the metadata produced by both types of attributes (predefined and custom) is accessed in exactly the same manner using reflection, something the following example demonstrates.

Custom Attribute Example

In this example, we will write a custom attribute that can be used in the following manner:

```
[HasBeenTested(50)]
class SomeClass { …
```

We want clients to be able to use this attribute to specify the extent to which a class or method has been tested. A value of 0 indicates that the entity has not been tested; 100 indicates complete and rigorous testing; and values in between indicate partial testing. We stipulate that this numerical value must be specified when using the attribute. In attribute terminology, this makes the numerical value a named parameter, which means it has to be specified when the attribute is used. We could also give the user the option to specify the name of the person who has tested the class or method:

```
[HasBeenTested(50, Tester="Alim Somani")]
```

This makes Tester a positional parameter, because its inclusion in the attribute declaration is optional. For the sake of simplicity, we will not leverage the positional capability in this example, but we will keep positional parameters in mind throughout our discussion.

Returning our attention to mandatory, named parameters, we might wonder how to inform the Runtime that our attribute must accept an integer when the attribute is declared. Recalling that all attributes are really classes that derive from System.Attribute, we can state the following axiom: *The named parameters for an attribute are the same as the parameters in the attribute class's constructor.*

Keeping the above comment in mind, we write our custom attribute in C#, whose source is in Listing 4.6. VB and managed C++ versions can be found at ☜ NET040008.

```
using System;

namespace TestAttribute
{
// Define the HasBeenTested attribute using AttributeUsage:
[AttributeUsage(AttributeTargets.Class|
  AttributeTargets.ClassMembers)]
public class HasBeenTested : Attribute {
  private int TestedLevel;
  public int GetConfidence() {return TestedLevel;}
```

```
// Constructor determines signature
public HasBeenTested(int TLevel) {TestedLevel=TLevel;}
public override string ToString() {
  if (TestedLevel == 0) {
    return "HasBeenTestedAttribute: " +
      "entity has not been tested.";
  } else if (TestedLevel == 100) {
    return "HasBeenTestedAttribute: " +
      "entity has been fully tested.";
  } else {
    return "HasBeenTestedAttribute: " +
      "entity has been partially tested.";
  }
}
}
}
```

Listing 4.6   Custom attribute, HasBeenTested.cs

The most important elements of the source have been highlighted. The first line in particular is likely to catch your attention:

```
[AttributeUsage(AttributeTargets.Class | AttributeTargets.ClassMembers)]
```

This may seem odd, but in order to inform the compiler that this class is really an attribute, you must precede its declaration with the AttributeUsage attribute. You may recognize that this puts us in the ironic position of having to use a predefined attribute to write our custom one.

AttributeUsage requires that we specify the entities on which the attribute can be used (classes, methods of classes, etc.) by employing the AttributeTargets enumeration found in the System namespace. We specify that our attribute can only be used on classes and their members by ORing those elements of the enumeration. In Visual Basic, this line would be equivalent to:

```
<AttributeUsage(AttributeTargets.Class OR AttributeTargets.ClassMembers)>
```

We could have optionally specified that our attribute may be used multiple times on the same class by using the AllowsMultiple parameter:

```
[AttributeUsage(AttributeTargets.Class, AllowsMultiple=true)]}
```

Recall our earlier discussion on attribute parameter types, and you will recognize that `AllowsMultiple` is a positional parameter because it is optional, whereas the first parameter (called `validon` in the MSDN) is a compulsory, named parameter. The `AttributeUsage` attribute exposes one other positional parameter, called `Inherited`, which determines whether the attribute will persist across inherited classes. Examples of these two parameters can be found at ^{CN}NET040009.

Turning our attention to the class constructor, we see that it accepts one integer parameter, informing the Runtime that the attribute has a single named integer parameter.

```
public HasBeenTested(int TLevel)
```

The remainder of the code is fairly straightforward: the public member variable `TestedLevel` allows clients to ascertain the level to which an entity has been tested, and the overridden `ToString()` method outputs a user-friendly message if the attribute is printed.

Compiling this listing with the C# compiler (csc /t:library HasBeenTested.cs) allows us to use the attribute from the second listing given below. VB and managed C++ equivalents can be found at ^{CN}NET040010.

```
using System;
using TestAttribute;

namespace TestClass {
  [Serializable] //system attribute
  [Obsolete("This class is outdated!")] //system attribute
  [HasBeenTested(44)] //a "custom" attribute we created
  public class Target {
    public void SomeFunction() {
      // SomeFunction code . . .
    }
  }
}
```

Listing 4.7   TargetClass.cs

In addition to our custom attribute, "HasBeenTested," we have applied two other predefined attributes on the `Target` class (Obsolete and Serializable) for comparative purposes. The Obsolete attribute can be used to inform clients that they are using an old version of the class, while the Serializable attribute indicates that the class can be packaged and sent to a remote location. We will revisit serialization in the Core Concepts section of Chapter 6.

Using the C# compiler again, we can produce a second assembly, called TestClass.DLL:

```
csc.exe /r:HasBeenTested.dll /t:library TargetClass.cs
```

This assembly is then used by the client program below, which utilizes reflection to inspect the Target class on which we have applied the HasBeenTested, CLSCompliant, and Serializable attributes.

```
using System;
using System.Reflection;
using TargetClass;
using TestAttribute;

class Test {
static void Main()
{
// Declare an instance of the Target class we used
// our custom attributes on:
Target tar = new Target();
attribute []attributes =
Attribute.GetCustomAttributes(tar.GetType());

Console.WriteLine("Custom attributes used on this type: {0}",
   attributes.Length);

// Interate through all the custom attributes defined
// on the Target class:
foreach (Attribute attrib in attributes) {

  // Print out the attribute:
  Console.WriteLine(attrib);

  // Is this attribute our custom one?
  // If so, we can print out additional information:
  if (attrib is HasBeenTested) {
    // This is our custom attribute.  Cast it, and
    // print out the level of testing that was done:
```

```
    HasBeenTested tested = (HasBeenTested)attrib;
    Console.WriteLine("Confidence Level: {0} / 100 ",
      tested.GetConfidence());
  }
}


}
}
```

Listing 4.8   TargetClient.cs

Again, the important lines of the program have been highlighted. The attributes of the Target class are ascertained using the `GetCustom` `Attributes()` method found in the `System.Attribute` class.

```
Target tar = new Target();
attribute[] attributes = Attribute.GetCustomAttributes(tar.GetType());
```

`GetCustomAttributes()` returns an array of `Attribute` classes, each of which represents a custom attribute that has been applied to the class. After printing out each attribute, the program checks to see whether it is our custom attribute:

```
  if (attrib is HasBeenTested) {
    HasBeenTested tested = (HasBeenTested)attrib;
```

The `is` keyword in C# can be used to test whether or not an expression can be successfully casted to the given type. In this case, we want to know whether the generic attribute is really our `HasBeenTested` attribute. If it is, then we cast it to an instance of the attribute so that we can garner the appropriate information from it.

If you compile this program from the command line:

```
csc.exe /r:TargetClass.dll /r:HasBeenTested.dll TargetClient.cs
```

---

you will see that applying the `Obsolete` system attribute on the Target class we are attempting to use manifests itself in the form of a compiler warning (this warning won't prevent you from running the code):

```
TargetClient.cs(12,19): warning CS0618: 'TargetClass.Target' is obsolete:
'This class is outdated!'
```

Running the TargetClient.exe application that is created produces the following output:

```
Custom attributes used on this type: 2
System.ObsoleteAttribute
HasBeenTestedAttribute: entity has been partially tested.
Confidence Level: 44 / 100
```

As can be seen, the program detected two custom attributes applied on the Target class, Obsolete and our attribute, HasBeenTested. Having detected that our custom attribute was applied to the class, the program prints out the degree to which the class has been tested.

Undoubtedly, many of you are wondering why we only picked up two custom attributes, although we applied three to the class. What happened to the Serializable attribute? To answer this question, use the ILDASM tool to inspect TargetClass.DLL. Examine its metadata using ILDASM and you will find the following information:

```
TypDefName: TargetClass.Target   (02000002)
Flags     : [Public] [AutoLayout] [Class] [Serializable]
CustomAttributeName: System.ObsoleteAttribute :: instance void
.ctor(class System.String)
ctor args: (This class is outdated!)


CustomAttribute #2 (0c000003)
---------------------------------
CustomAttributeName: TestAttribute.HasBeenTested :: instance void
.ctor(int32)
ctor args: (44)
```

The metadata above shows that the Serializable attribute did not generate a new section of metadata as did Obsolete and HasBeenTested; it simply appended metadata to the [Flags] section of the class. Because of this, Serializable belongs to a small family of attributes referred to as "pseudo attributes," which, unlike their bona fide counterparts, do not add a CustomAttribute section of metadata to the assembly. Thus, pseudo attributes cannot be picked up by the reflection technique. For a list of the pseudo attributes in the Runtime classes, see ᴄᴺ⟩NET040011.

This is the exception to our generalization that all predefined attributes are really custom attributes. And in case you are wondering, at the time of this writing, you cannot write a "custom-pseudo" attribute.

From the metadata above, we can see that attributes are nothing more than classes with their construction arguments embedded into an assembly's metadata. When a client application uses a type that has attributes applied on it, the CLR uses this metadata to instantiate the attribute classes so that they can be accessed through reflection. In our example, the sequence of events would proceed like this:

1. The client application uses the Target class found in TargetClass .DLL.
2. The CLR examines the metadata in TargetClass.DLL, and determines that two attributes were applied on the Target class: Obsolete and HasBeenTested.
3. The CLR retrieves the constructor arguments from the assembly's metadata, and instantiates each attribute class as follows:
   a. Obsolete("This class is outdated")
   b. HasBeenTested(44)
4. These instantiated classes can now be retrieved and inspected using the GetCustomAttributes() method.

HOW DO I/WHY DO I?

How Do I Write a Custom Attribute with Positional (Optional) Parameters?

To give a custom attribute positional parameters, you must give the attribute a class public member variable or property with the same name as the positional parameter.

Assume that we wanted to give the HasBeenTested attribute an optional Tester parameter, as shown below:

```
[HasBeenTested(50, Tester="Bill Baldasti")]
```

To accomplish this, the HasBeenTested class must expose a public member string or property called Tester. Source code for the HasBeenTested attribute with this added capability can be found at ⌕NET040012.

Can I Have Multiple Constructors in my Attribute Class?

Your attribute class (like any class) can have multiple constructors that accept different arguments. Remember that a constructor defines the named (mandatory) parameters of an attribute. This means that you can use multiple constructors to give an attribute multiple named parameter setups. We could, for example, stipulate that our HasBeenClass must accept either a number or a string by writing two equivalent constructors. Examples of this approach can be found at ⌕NET040013.

SUMMARY

Reflection allows access to an assembly's metadata by using the classes found in the System.Reflection namespace. This can be the standard metadata produced by IL-compiler to describe the types contained in an assembly, or the metadata that is embedded by a predefined or custom attribute.

Using reflection, one can traverse through the .NET entity hierarchy (AppDomain → Assembly → Module → Class etc.), ascertaining information about the types one is interested in, and invoking them, if desired. The reverse process is facilitated by the classes found in the System.Reflection.Emit namespace, whereby .NET entities can be constructed dynamically in memory, and invoked.

Custom attributes are classes that inherit from the System.Attribute class, and can be used by developers to extend an assembly's metadata for their own purposes.

Topic: Delegates

Asynchronous notification schemes are incredibly efficient. If you call a friend and he or she is not home, you don't wait on the line for hours to speak with them. Most often, you leave your phone number with the person on the line, so that when your friend does get home, she can notify you of her arrival by calling you back. By not waiting idly on the line for an extended period of time, you are free to do other things.

Callback functions facilitate exactly this type of asynchronous behavior. When calling a class's method (your friend's telephone number), you provide it with a callback function (your telephone number) so that you can be alerted when a particular event occurs (your friend returns home). As a result of this exchange, your program (you) is free to do other things in the interim.

Callback functions are equivalent to function pointers in C and C++, and the AddressOf operator in Visual Basic. All of these constructs serve the same purpose—to provide the address of a method (phone number) that should be called back when an event occurs. The problem with callback functions was that they did not communicate parameter/return value information, or guarantees about where they pointed. In other words, the person taking down your phone number could not verify that it was in the proper format, or even existed.

In the .NET Framework, callback functions have evolved into delegates. Delegates differ from callback functions in three respects:

- They are type-safe, which means that they make guarantees about the parameters they expect (the phone number is in the correct format).
- The CLR will always ensure that they point to a valid function or class method (the phone number exists).
- They allow for multicasting, which means that you can specify a chain of functions in one or many different objects and locations that should be called back. This would be equivalent to leaving numerous phone numbers at your friend's place, and having him call all of them back when he got home.

Delegates must derive from the `System.MulticastDelegate` class, and wrap the callback functions you specify. By acting as a buffer between the real callback function and its caller, they can provide the guarantees and services listed above.

Delegates also remove one notable limitation of C++ function pointers and the AddressOf operator: they can point to a class's methods, whereas traditional callback schemes only allow global functions to be used. You may be wondering how delegates handle a scenario where a callback class has been deallocated. Remember, because both the class and delegate are running within the CLR, such a situation will never occur—the class will never be garbage-collected if a delegate is wrapping one of its methods.

EXAMPLE

Continuing with our phone number analogy, we consider the C# class below, which will call back a client if he provides it with a "PhoneNumber" delegate. Managed C++ and VB.NET examples can be found at ☁NET040014.

```
using System;

namespace CallBackExample {
public class CallBack {

  // In order to be called back, clients must provide
  // the following delegate to the CallMyFriend() method.
  public delegate void PhoneNumber(String message);

  // To be called back, clients run the following
  // method, providing the PhoneNumber delegate where
```

```
// they can be called back.
public void CallMyFriend(PhoneNumber wakeupFunc) {
  // Friend is home, call back:
  wakeupFunc("I just got home, you called?");
}
}
}
```

Listing 4.9   Callback class

Saving the code above as CallBack.cs, we produce an assembly in the usual manner:

```
csc.exe /t:library CallBack.cs
```

To use this class, clients construct a PhoneNumber delegate (something we'll demonstrate in a moment) and pass it to the CallMyFriend() method. When our friend arrives home (triggering the event), the method calls the delegate:

```
wakeupFunc("I just got home, you called?");
```

Remember that delegates are really classes deriving from System .MulticastDelegate. This being the case, it doesn't seem as if the line above should compile; you can't invoke a class in such a manner. What you're seeing, however, is some trickery by the IL-compiler. Behind the scenes it is calling the Invoke() method of System.MulticastDelegate, which calls whatever function the delegate wraps. You can confirm this by using ILDASM to inspect the generated IL code.

Having compiled the CallBack class, we can use the delegate with the following C# code:

```
using System;
using CallBackExample;

public class MyClass  {

  // This function will be called when our friend
  // calls back:
  static void MyPhoneNumber(String s)   {
    // Print out what our friend says:
    Console.WriteLine(S);
```

```
      Console.WriteLine("Thanks for calling me back!");
   }

   public static int Main() {
     CallBack cBack;
     cBack = new CallBack();

     // Before calling our friend, we must construct a
     // delegate that is passed to the CallMyFriend() method.
     CallBack.PhoneNumber PhoneNum;
     PhoneNum = new CallBack.PhoneNumber(MyPhoneNumber);

     // Call our friend and pass it the PhoneNum
     // delegate so he can call us back:
     cBack.CallMyFriend(PhoneNum);
     return 0;
   }
}
```

Listing 4.10   C# client delegate code

The Visual Basic syntax differs significantly in that you must use the
AddressOf operator:

```
imports System
imports CallBackExample

Module MyApp

  'Our callback function:
  Sub MyPhoneNumber(ByVal s As String)
      System.Console.WriteLine(s)
      System.Console.WriteLine("Thanks for calling me back!")
  End Sub

  Sub Main
    dim cBack as CallBack
    cBack = new CallBack()   'Remember, no Set!

    'Construct the delegate:
    dim PhoneNum as CallBack.PhoneNumber
    PhoneNum = _
      new CallBack.PhoneNumber(AddressOf MyPhoneNumber)
```

```
' Call our friend and pass it the PhoneNum
' delegate so he can call us back:
cBack.CallMyFriend(PhoneNum)

End Sub
End Module
```

Listing 4.11   Visual Basic client delegate code

The highlighted lines in both listings illustrate that a delegate must be constructed before it can be passed to the CallMyFriend() method. When creating an instance of the delegate, you must pass it the address of the function it will wrap. Note that in Visual Basic you must use the AddressOf operator to do this, whereas in C# you do not. Also note that the function the delegate is wrapping must accept the same parameters and have the same return value as the delegate itself. If the C# client method MyPhoneNumber() had accepted an integer instead of a string, the compiler would have informed you that:

```
CallBackClient.cs(23,39): error CS0123: Method
'MyClass.MyPhoneNumber(int)' does not match delegate 'void
CallBackExample.CallBack.PhoneNumber(string)'
```

Compiling and Running the Example
Compiling each listing with its respective compiler:

```
csc.exe /r:CallBack.dll CallBackClient.cs
vbc.exe /r:CallBack.dll CallBackClient.vb
```

produces two applications that produce the following output:

```
I just got home, you called?
Thanks for calling me back!
```

You could argue (correctly) that the Callback class presented in Listing 4.9 does not really facilitate asynchronous notification. Both client applications call the CallMyFriend() function, which immediately calls back the delegate it has been provided with. It would be like calling a friend and then having him call back immediately on another line without having hung up on the first one.

To provide truly asynchronous behavior, CallMyFriend() should return immediately to the client and then call the delegate at some point after that. This is a more involved procedure and requires using another thread in the Callback class. For the sake of brevity, we have omitted this more complex approach. However, a truly asynchronous Callback class can be found at ⊶ NET040015.

DELEGATE CHAINS

One of the most powerful features of delegates is that they can wrap a "chain" of functions, all of which will be called when the delegate is invoked. This is accomplished by using the static Combine() method of the Delegate class found in the Runtime library. The VB snippet below demonstrates this procedure. The complete client source can be found at ⊶ NET040016.

```
'Callback function 1:
Sub MyPhoneNumber1(ByVal s As String)
  System.Console.WriteLine(s)
  System.Console.WriteLine("Friend 1: Thanks for calling back!")
End Sub


'Callback function 2:
Sub MyPhoneNumber2(ByVal s As String)
  System.Console.WriteLine(s)
  System.Console.WriteLine("Friend 2: Thanks for calling back!")
End Sub


'Construct a delegate that wraps the chain of
'functions: MyPhoneNumber1 and MyPhoneNumber2
dim PhoneNum1, PhoneNum2 as CallBack.PhoneNumber
dim PhoneChain as CallBack.PhoneNumber
PhoneNum1 = new CallBack.PhoneNumber(AddressOf MyPhoneNumber1)
PhoneNum2 = new CallBack.PhoneNumber(AddressOf MyPhoneNumber2)
PhoneChain = System.Delegate.Combine(PhoneNum1,PhoneNum2)


'Call our friend, passing him the delegate that
'now wraps the chain of functions.
'cBack is an instance of the class in listing 4.9
'(see full source online)
cBack.CallMyFriend(PhoneChain)
```

Listing 4.12 Constructing delegate chains in VB.NET

As the highlighted code in Listing 4.12 depicts, a delegate that wraps a chain of functions is constructed and passed to the CallMyFriend() method. If you are wondering why we constructed the chain using

System.Delegate.Combine() instead of Delegate.Combine(), it is because the latter statement creates a syntactical dilemma for the VB compiler due to the Delegate's keyword designation in the language (VB can't handle having "Delegate" as both a system level class instance and a keyword used for creating new classes).

In C#, the construction of delegate chains is syntactically cleaner because the compiler overloads the + operator for the delegate class, as shown in the partial client listing below. The full version can be found at ⊶ NET040017.

```
// This function will be called when our friend
// calls back:
static void MyPhoneNumber1(string s) {
  Console.WriteLine(s);
  Console.WriteLine("Friend 1: Thanks for calling me back!");
}

static void MyPhoneNumber2(string s) {
  Console.WriteLine(s);
  Console.WriteLine("Friend 2: Thanks for calling me back!");
}

// Construct a delegate that wraps the chain of
// functions: MyPhoneNumber1 and MyPhoneNumber2
// Note use of the "+" operator
CallBack.PhoneNumber PhoneChain;
PhoneChain = new CallBack.PhoneNumber(MyPhoneNumber1);
PhoneChain += new CallBack.PhoneNumber(MyPhoneNumber2);

// Call our friend, passing him the delegate that
// now wraps the chain of functions.
cBack.CallMyFriend(PhoneChain);
```

Listing 4.13   Constructing delegate chains in C#

You can, if you want, use the Combine() method to construct delegate chains in C#, just as we did in Visual Basic. In fact, this is what the C# compiler is doing behind the scenes when you use the + operator. Inspecting the IL code of the program above using ILDASM confirms this.

Running the Code
Compiling and running either of the client programs given above results in the following output:

```
I just got home, you called?
Friend 1: Thanks for calling me back!
I just got home, you called?
Friend 2: Thanks for calling me back!
```

Keep in mind that the `CallMyFriend()` method that actually invokes the delegate has no idea that it is calling a chain of functions. As you will recall from our earlier discussion, the IL compiler is calling the delegate's `Invoke()` method behind the scenes. At this point the CLR intercedes, determines that the delegate wraps a chain of functions, and calls them accordingly.

Just as you can add a function to the chain using the `Combine()` method, you can remove one using the `Remove()` method. Not surprisingly, the "-" operator in C# can be used as a shortcut. Examples of removing functions from the chain can be found at ⊶⁽ᶜᴺ⁾NET040018.

VISUAL BASIC EVENTS

Note: This discussion is intended primarily for VB6 developers, although developers unfamiliar with events in VB6 should still be able to follow it.

Visual Basic 6 is an event-driven programming language. A large portion of VB development consists of writing code to handle events that are raised by the objects in one's application. If you wanted to display a message box when a button is clicked, for example, you would insert the following code in the button's click event:

```
Private Sub Button1_Click()
  MsgBox ("Button was clicked.")
End Sub
```

Listing 4.14   Responding to a button click in Visual Basic 6

`Button1_Click` is called an event handler, because it handles the button's click event. It is important to realize that you rarely call the button's event handler directly from your application. The VB Runtime automatically invokes `Button1_Click` for you when the button is clicked.

Starting with Visual Basic 5, VB classes have been able to expose their own events using the `Events` and `RaiseEvents` keywords. By exposing an event, you invite clients to write code that would be invoked when the event occurred. This is best illustrated by the example below. (The complete source code can also be found online at ⟨CN⟩NET040019.)

Raising Events

Consider the VB6 StockInfo class in Listing 4.15, which exposes a single event:

```
Public Event PriceChanged(ByVal price As Double)

Public Sub Start()
   'Loop continually and trigger the PriceChanged
   'event with a random price every 5 seconds.
   Do
      'Delay for 5 seconds.
       before = Timer
      Do
        DoEvents
      Loop Until Timer - before > 5

      'Raise the event, which will trigger any
      'client code associated PriceChanged
      RaiseEvent PriceChanged(rnd*100)
   Loop
End Sub
```

Listing 4.15   VB6 StockInfo class

The StockInfo class exposes one event called PriceChanged. Clients write code for this event (we will see how momentarily), which is triggered when we raise the event using the RaiseEvent keyword. The idea behind events is similar to the premise delegates: by "subscribing" to our event, a client is free to do other things until the event is raised. (The relationship between delegates and events is explained in the following section, Events and Delegates.)

Listening to Events

If we were writing a client that wanted to subscribe to the PriceChanged event shown in Listing 4.15, we would declare an instance of the class using the WithEvents keyword (this is VB6 code; we will examine changes in VB.NET momentarily):

```
dim WithEvents stck As StockInfo
```

Because we used the WithEvents keyword when declaring the StockInfo class, we can now write the code shown in Listing 4.16, which will be called whenever the class's PriceChanged method is raised. Our subroutine must be called stck_PriceChanged, because in VB6 event handlers must adhere to the following naming convention: ObjectName_EventName.

```
Private Sub stck_PriceChanged(ByVal price As Double)
    'Print out the stock price in the Debug Window
    Debug.Print price
End Sub
```

Listing 4.16   Attaching event code with the PriceChanged event

As a result of the code in Listing 4.16, any time the PriceChanged event is raised by our component, the stock price will be printed in VB6's environment debug window. Look back at Listing 4.15 and you will see that the PriceChanged event is repeatedly raised after we call the class's Start() method. This method loops forever and raises the PriceChanged event with a random price every five seconds. In reality, it would probably do something more sophisticated, such as query a live stock feed and raise the event when the stock price changed. If we were to add the following line of code to our VB6 project (in the form's Load() method, for example), the PriceChanged event would be raised every five seconds.

```
Set stck = New StockInfo
stck.Start
```

If you were to run the application (again, full source at ᶜᴺ⟩NET040020), the VB6 Debug window would display a new stock price every 5 seconds, as shown in Figure 4.1.

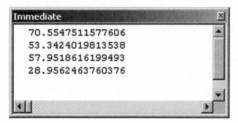

Figure 4.1   PriceChanged event raised every 5 seconds

VB.NET EVENTS

Writing a class that exposes an event in VB.NET is very similar to doing the same in VB6. You use the `event` keyword to declare the event, then use the `RaiseEvent` keyword to trigger it. Listing 4.17 illustrates the StockInfo class rewritten in VB.NET (source also available at ᴄᴺ NET040021).

```
Class StockInfo

  public event PriceChanged(ByVal price as double)
  public sub Start()
    'For simplicity, just raise the event once, although
    'in reality we would loop continually and raise the
    'event whenever the stock price changed.
    RaiseEvent PriceChanged(100.00)
  end sub
end Class
```

Listing 4.17   StockInfo class in VB.NET

As with the VB6 code in Listing 4.15, Listing 4.17 exposes a `PriceChanged` event that clients subscribe to when they wish to be notified that the stock price has changed. Subscribing to an event in VB.NET is a little different than VB6. You still declare a class using the `WithEvents` keyword:

```
public WithEvents stck as StockInfo
```

What changes, however, is the name of the associated event handler. Recall from Listing 4.17 that VB6 events handlers must follow the naming convention `ObjectName_EventName`, which was why our event handler had to be called `Stck_PriceChanged`. In VB.NET, you can call your event handler whatever you like, but you must associate it with the class's event using a new keyword, `Handles`.

```
private sub MyPriceChanged(Byval price as double)
Handles stck.PriceChanged
  Console.WriteLine("Stock Price: {0}",price)
end sub
```

Listing 4.18   Writing event handler code using the Handles keyword in VB.NET

As a result of Listing 4.18, whenever the StockInfo `PriceChanged` event is raised, our `MyPriceChanged` method will be called implicitly. VB.NET has an additional capability as well—you can write multiple event handlers for a single event. Thus we could also write the following code, which also responds to the PriceChanged event.

```
private sub MyPriceChanged2(Byval price as double)
Handles stck.PriceChanged
  'Do something with the Stock Price
end sub
```

Listing 4.19   Writing another event handler in VB.NET

Now, both the MyPriceChanged and MyPriceChanged2 methods will be invoked whenever StockInfo's PriceChanged event is raised. This cannot be done in Visual Basic 6.

EVENTS AND DELEGATES

Events and delegates both function in a similar manner: they both allow a component to asynchronously notify a client that something important has occurred (a stock price has changed, a database has been updated, etc.). But delegates are, in fact, the underlying architecture *behind* VB.NET events. When you use the event, RaiseEvents, and WithEvents keywords in VB.NET (as we did in the previous example), the VB.NET compiler translates your event statements into delegate equivalents behind the scenes.

If you are developing solely in VB.NET, you can use VB.NET events as we have illustrated and let the VB.NET compiler take care of the details. If you wish to write events in C# or managed C++, however, you are not afforded such abstraction and must understand the relationship between events and delegates in the .NET Framework. To this end, we will demonstrate how to write the StockInfo info class in C#, where we must use the underlying delegate directly. This C# example can also be found online at ⊶**CN**⧽NET040022.

The relationship between delegates and events is best understood if you consider the VB.NET code in Listing 4.17. Consider the line that declares the PriceChanged event:

```
public event PriceChanged(ByVal price as double)
```

This line states that the StockInfo class exposes an event called PriceChanged, which contains a parameter called price (of type double). When the event is raised, the price variable contains some value that the client is (presumably) interested in.

In C#, as in VB.NET, you still use the event keyword to expose an event (as we will see in Listing 4.21). But in C#, what precedes the event keyword must be a delegate that takes two parameters:

```
public delegate void PriceChangedDelegate(Object o, PriceEventArgs p);
```

The first parameter of the delegate (Object) contains the object that invoked the event (this is equivalent to whatever object called RaiseEvent in VB.NET, which would be the StockInfo class itself). The second parameter, a class that inherits from System.EventArgs, is a class that contains any information the event must communicate. In our case, our event must communicate a double parameter called price, and even though price is simply a double, we will still need to construct a class called "price" that will house the double as a public member variable. (It is possible for the second parameter of an event delegate to be a single variable such as a string or integer, but the convention is that it be a class inheriting from System.EventArgs.)

The important thing to realize when using events in C# is, again, that event parameters are communicated through a single class that contains public member variables corresponding to the event parameters. For example, our event could communicate two parameters (a stock symbol and a stock price):

```
public event PriceChanged(ByVal price as double, _
  symbol as string)
```

In that case we would need a class with two public member variables: price and symbol. Since we only need to communicate one parameter, however, all we need is a class that inherits from System.EventArgs, with a public member variable called Price. Create a new C# file (call it StockInfo.cs) and add the code in Lisitng 4.20 to it.

```
public class PriceEventArgs : System.EventArgs
{
  public double Price;
  public PriceEventArgs(double StockPrice)
  {
    Price=StockPrice;
  }
}
```

Listing 4.20   The PriceEventArgs class

The PriceEventArgs class in Listing 4.20 is straightforward: it contains a public variable called Price that can be set in the class's constructor. Having written a class that inherits from System.EventArgs, we now declare a delegate that accepts this class as its second parameter:

```
public delegate void PriceChangedDelegate(Object o, PriceEventArgs p);
```

Think about what a client could do if called back with such a delegate. First, the client could determine who invoked the delegate by inspecting the Object parameter. Second, the client could scrutinize the PriceEventArgs class, which happens to contain a member variable called Price (this is why the Price variable has to be public in Listing 4.20—so that clients can retrieve it).

We can now write a StockInfo class in C#, similar to the VB.NET version in Listing 4.17. There are a couple of differences, however. First, what follows the event keyword is the PriceChangedDelegate we just created—not a method with parameters, as in the VB.NET example. Second, our class does not use RaiseEvent to trigger the event but must explicitly invoke the delegate. These differences are highlighted in Listing 4.21.

```
public class Stockinfo
{
  public event PriceChangedDelegate PriceChanged;
  public void Start()
  {
    // Invoke the delegate.  This takes the place
    // of RaiseEvent in VB.NET:
    PriceEventArgs price = new PriceEventArgs(100.00);
    PriceChanged(this,price);
  }

}
```

Listing 4.21   The StockInfo class written in C#

The StockInfo class in Listing 4.21 is functionally identical to the VB.NET version in Listing 4.17: it exposes a PriceChanged event that is invoked when the class's Start() method is called. You can compile this class into a DLL assembly using the C# compiler:

```
csc.exe /t:library StockInfo.cs
```

The C# compiler will produce a file called StockInfo.DLL, which you can now use from Visual Basic, as depicted in Listing 4.22.

```
module Example
  private WithEvents stck as StockInfo
  private sub OnPriceChange(Byval o as object, _
    byval p as PriceEventArgs) Handles stck.PriceChanged
    System.Console.WriteLine("Stock Price: {0}",p.Price)
  end sub

  sub main
    stck = new Stockinfo
    stck.Start()
  end sub
end module
```

Listing 4.22   Using the C# StockInfo class from VB.NET

The VB.NET program uses the C# StockInfo class, much like the VB.NET one: it associates an event handler with the class's PriceChanged event using the Handles keyword, and then calls the class's Start() method, which triggers the event. The important difference is that the OnPriceChange event handler does not receive a price parameter (as it does in Listing 4.18). Instead, it receives an instance of the PriceEventArgs class, whose public member variables it can scrutinize for information.

Look at listing 4.22 and you will notice that even though we explicitly used delegates in the C# StockInfo class, we are completely abstracted from them in VB.NET. This prompts us to make the following concluding observations:

• When you declare an event in a VB.NET class, the VB.NET compiler converts it into a corresponding delegate behind the scenes.
• When you use RaiseEvent in VB.NET, the compiler implicitly invokes the underlying event delegate.
• When you use Handles in VB.NET, the compiler is really registering your method with the underlying event delegate, so that your method is invoked with the delegate called.

As can be seen, delegates are the underlying mechanism behind VB.NET events. Those familiar with COM will note that this marks the end of the ConnectionPoint mechanism that drove events in VB6.

HOW AND WHY

Can Delegates Be Used for Anything Besides Callbacks?

Even though delegates are the mechanism behind callbacks in the .NET Framework, there is no stipulation that they be used only for this purpose. Delegates can be useful in multicast/subscription situations, where the number of functions triggered by an event can change dynamically. See ∘**CN**⟩NET040023 for an example that uses delegates in this manner.

What Is the System.MulticastDelegate GetInvocationList() Method Used For?

In our example, the PhoneNumber delegate did not have a return value. Consider what would happen if it did. The `CallMyFriend()` method would invoke the delegate as follows:

```
someResult = wakeupFunc("I just got home, you called?");
```

The delegate would invoke the function it wrapped and propagate whatever value the function returned to someResult. If the delegate wrapped a chain function, however, the return value of the last function in the chain would be stored into someResult, while the rest would be discarded. This behavior is not always desirable. We might want someResult to store some combination of the values returned by the functions wrapped by the delegate. `GetInvocationList()` is designed to address this situation.

The `GetInvocationList()` method can be used to retrieve the chain of functions that a delegate wraps. Once retrieved, each function can be called individually and its return value can be manipulated as desired. An illustration of the use of the `GetInvocationList()` method can be found at ∘**CN**⟩NET040024.

SUMMARY

Delegates are classes that inherit from `System.MulticastDelegate` and encapsulate one or more functions or class methods. The functions wrapped by a delegate must match the return value and arguments of the delegate signature. The `Combine()` and `Remove()` methods of a delegate class can be used to add and remove the functions it wraps. When you invoke a delegate, you implicitly invoke its contained functions.

Delegates are used in the .NET Framework in place of callback functions (function pointers in C++, AddressOf in Visual Basic). By acting as a buffer between functions and their callers, delegate classes can ensure that callbacks are performed in a type-safe manner. The ability of delegates to be used for callbacks and to wrap multiple functions allows for a phenomenon known as multicasting, whereby one source notifies numerous functions of a given event.

Finally, delegates are now the underlying mechanism behind events in VB.NET. With VB.NET, you can still use the Visual Basic 6 events and RaiseEvents keywords to expose events in your classes, but you must use the new Handles keyword to write VB.NET event handlers. Behind the scenes, VB.NET translates your event statements into delegates, which are used by the .NET Runtime to trigger events and invoke their event handlers. You can also expose events in C# and managed C++ classes, but you must explicitly write and manage the underlying delegate.

Topic: Garbage Collection

Like a Java Virtual Machine, the CLR removes the burden of memory management from developers by destroying objects once they are no longer being referenced. For years, Visual Basic programmers were afforded this service by the VB runtime, and this luxury is now inherent in any language that targets the CLR.

Before an object is removed from memory, it must free any resources it has allocated during its lifetime. In C++, this "cleanup code" is usually housed in an object's destructor, whereas in VB it is placed in the Class Terminate() method. Under the .NET Framework, cleanup code must reside in an object's Finalize() method, which is called just before the object is garbage-collected by the CLR.

Finalize() is a method in the System.Object class from which all other .NET classes derive. You only have to override this method when you have cleanup code that should be performed before the class is destroyed.

For C++ developers, implementing this change is not as painful as it may seem. You still write destructors in the standard manner you always did, as the managed C++ code below illustrates. (Note that in C# you also use this destructor syntax.)

```
__gc public class MyObject
{
  ~MyObject ()
  {
    // My cleanup code goes here.
```

```
    }
};
```

Behind the scenes, the compiler has taken the code in the destructor and placed it in the class's `Finalize()` method. Nevertheless, the intended behavior is the same—the cleanup code is called just before the object is destroyed. The compiler will also mimic destructor behavior in one other respect: if your class has inherited another class, the compiler will insert code to call the base class's `Finalize()` method after your cleanup code has executed. This would be equivalent to having a class's destructor call its parent destructor once it had executed.

In managed C++ and C#, you *must* use this destructor syntax (you cannot write a `Finalize()` method). In Visual Basic you must be more explicit, as the following code reveals (note that you must use the `overrides` keyword, which is used to override the methods of inherited classes).

```
Class MyObject

    protected overrides sub Finalize()
      'Place VB cleanup code here
    end Sub
end Class
```

GARBAGE COLLECTION TIMING

From these examples, it would seem that the new destruction scheme in the .NET Framework is nothing more than a syntax shuffle, one that C++ and C# programmers don't even have to be aware of, given that their compilers mask such details. Unfortunately, this is not the case. For although it is true that objects are destroyed when they are no longer being referenced, under the .NET Framework there is no guarantee as to when this will actually happen. If the processor's workload is heavy, the garbage collector may not get around to destroying an object until long after it has no longer been referenced. If the object has allocated expensive resources, it will hold on to them for this extended period of time. This unpredictable behavior is referred to as *nondeterministic finalization*.

Although nondeterministic finalization is the price paid for having memory managed by the CLR, objects that have allocated expensive resources (database connections, communication channels) should be able to release them in a more timely manner. Microsoft's solution is to have you expose a method that clients explicitly call when they are finished using your object. By placing cleanup code in this method, as opposed to Finalize(), resources can be freed immediately and do not depend upon the next execution of the garbage collector. Under the .NET Framework, the convention is to call this method Dispose(), although you can certainly name it something else (Close, Release, etc.).

The problem with this approach is that you are left in the precarious position of hoping that clients call your Dispose() method. If they do not, expensive resources will never be freed, which can be as problematic as the original dilemma of having them freed in an untimely fashion. Microsoft anticipated this situation as well, and the "solution to their solution" requires using the SuppressFinalization() method found in the System.GC class.

Under this approach, objects have two methods that free resources: Dispose() and Finalize(). Depending upon the client's actions, resource deallocation can proceed in one of two ways:

1. The client calls Dispose(): Dispose() releases the object's resources and calls GC.SuppressFinalization(), informing the CLR that Finalize() should not be called.
2. The client forgets to call Dispose(): when the object is garbage-collected the CLR calls Finalize(), which releases the object's resources.

The following Visual Basic code demonstrates this hybrid approach. Managed C++ and C# examples can be found at ⌗NET040025.

```
Class MyObject
  private Sub CleanUp
    'Cleanup resources here
  end sub

  public Sub Dispose()
    'Free resources:
    CleanUp()
    'No need for CLR to call Finalize:
    GC.SuppressFinalize(me)
  end sub

  protected overrides sub Finalize()
    'Client did not call Dispose!, free resources:
    CleanUp()
```

```
end Sub
end Class
```

Listing 4.23   Using Finalize and Dispose

The `GC.SuppressFinalize(me)` line informs the CLR that this object has released its resources and it should not call `Finalize()`. The `me` construct in Visual Basic is the equivalent to `this` in C++ and C#; it refers to the current instance the method is executing on.

In addition to guarding against the client's failure to call `Dispose()`, as we do here, you should also be able to handle clients that call your `Dispose()` method multiple times. In the preceding code, this would translate into determining whether resources have already been freed in the `CleanUp()` method.

Garbage Collection and Performance

If you are not careful, finalization can significantly degrade performance. If a client instantiates a five-thousand-element array of finalizable objects, for example, the garbage collector must call `Finalize()` explicitly against every element. Because of this, finalizable objects are typically destroyed later than their nonfinalizable equivalents. A byproduct of this demoted status is that finalizable objects can unnecessarily prolong the destruction of other objects to which they have references.

For performance reasons, the `Finalize()` method should only be employed when efficiently freeing a particular resource is a prime concern. Also, the `Finalize()` method cannot make any assumptions about the thread on which it executes, because it is called by the CLR's garbage-collection thread. Thus, it cannot access thread-local storage (TLS).

Finally, if you expose a `Dispose()` method that clients call to explicitly free your object's resources, you should prepare for the possibility that they might call it numerous times.

HOW AND WHY

Can I Prevent an Object from Being Destroyed in Its Finalize() Method?

The CLR garbage collects objects when they are no longer being referenced. It is possible (although unlikely) to establish a reference to the object in its own `Finalize()` method. This could involve setting some global variable to the object instance, as demonstrated by the following VB code:

```
protected overrides sub
Finalize()
  someGlobalVariable = me
end Sub
```

As a result of this assignment, a reference to the object now exists, and it can no longer be collected. The object has thus gone through the unique cycle of having been alive, then deemed OK to be destroyed (dead), then becoming alive again. This fortunate change in the object's fate is called resurrection. Information on this advanced and rarely used technique can be found at ‿NET040026.

Is There a Way I Can Force the Garbage Collector to Destroy Outstanding Objects?

Although the CLR will automatically run the Garbage Collector from time to time, you can run it explicitly by using the GC.Collect() method found in the Runtime classes.

Can I Declare Types That Are Not Garbage Collected?

This is only an option for managed C++ developers, who can place the __nogc expression in front of types so that they won't fall prey to the CLR's garbage collector when no longer being referenced. See ‿NET040027 for examples of the __nogc expression. Another option to forego garbage collection is to write native code and then call it from the .NET environment, a topic addressed in Chapter 5.

SUMMARY

Objects that require explicit notification of their destruction by the CLR's garbage collector must implement the Finalize() method. In C# and managed C++, any class destructors you write will be automatically replaced with this method by their respective compilers. This convenience is not afforded to Visual Basic developers, who must explicitly replace their Class Terminate() subroutines with Finalize(). Although the Garbage Collector will call an object's Finalize() method after it has last been referenced, it makes no guarantee about the time between these two events. As a result, objects that have allocated resources may hold onto them well after the object is no longer being used. Microsoft suggests writing an additional method called Dispose(), which clients call explicitly once an object is no longer being used. If the client calls Dispose(), Dispose() releases the objects resources and calls GC.SuppressFinalization() so that Finalize() is not called by the CLR when the object is collected. If the client forgets to call Dispose(), the CLR calls Finalize() when the object is garbage-collected, and resources are freed.

Chapter Summary

In this chapter we examined the various language features in the .NET Framework. We first looked at attributes, which are nonprogrammatic code statements that influence application behavior by embedding additional metadata into an assembly. An assembly's metadata can be retrieved using reflection, the second topic of this chapter. Reflection can be used when you have no prior knowledge of an assembly and wish to use its classes dynamically at runtime.

Delegates are the .NET equivalents of C/C++ functions pointers and are most often used to facilitate asynchronous notification between a component and client. Delegates are also the mechanism behind VB.NET's event model, marking the end of the COM ConnectionPoint model that drove events in VB6.

The final topic of this chapter, Garbage Collection, is a service afforded to all programs executing within the CLR. Garbage collection presents some new issues for developers, most notably for C and C++ programmers who were previously burdened with the responsibility of memory management. Objects that wish to release resources before they are garbage-collected must implement a special method called Finalize().

In the following chapters we will see some of the these language features in practice. Attributes, for example, will be used in the next chapter to call Win32 DLL functions from the managed environment, as well as to give classes the transactional capabilities discussed in Chapter 6. We will revisit delegates in Chapter 7, when we look at Windows Forms, the new way to design Win32 screens in the .NET Framework.

Chapter 5

—

MIGRATING NATIVE CODE TO .NET

A natural question for many developers, given the advent of .NET, is the impending status of widespread technologies such as COM and plain Win32 DLLs. Unlike the .NET Framework, these older technologies produce native code that runs outside the realm of the CLR. The .NET Framework would be of little value if developers were forced to abandon their existing components and frameworks. Clearly, there must be some way to integrate code from these two different worlds.

In this chapter we will examine the two .NET technologies that allow native code to be called from the managed environment. The first, called Platform Invocation Services (PInvoke for short) allows managed applications to call functions exposed by Win32 DLLs. The second, termed COM Interop, allows these same applications to transparently use unmanaged COM components. Yet a third technique is a feature of Microsoft's next version of Visual C++, called VC.NET. This development tool allows one to write native and managed code in the same source file, while the compiler performs the necessary conversions behind the scenes. Information on VC.NET's native code capabilities can be found at ⌖NET050021.

Regardless of the mechanism used to call native code from the managed realm, a performance hit is incurred, as the CLR must suspend its execution and give way to code that operates outside its boundaries. It must also "translate" the exchange of data from both sides of the fence using a process called "marshaling." For this reason, it is a wise practice to develop new code exclusively in the .NET Runtime and limit the use of native APIs wherever possible.

In addition to allowing native code to be invoked from the managed environment, the .NET Framework also permits the reverse, allowing managed code to be called from the unmanaged realm. This is accomplished either by using the managed form of C-style callback functions called delegates that we saw in Chapter 4, or by using a feature of the COM Interop called COM Callable Wrappers (CCWs). We will investigate both methods in this chapter.

CORE CONCEPTS

Unsafe Code

Some of you may be aware of the `unsafe` keyword in C#, which allows the use of pointers and gives rise to something called "unsafe code." You might imagine that these unsafe regions are yet another way to call native code in the managed environment. This is not, however, the case. To understand why requires making a subtle distinction in the .NET terminology, which can be confusing.

Native code is machine code that exists in a binary format that can be read directly by the processor (hence the term *native*). Win32 DLLs and COM components are compiled to this type of code. Native code is said to run in the "unmanaged" environment because it executes outside the boundaries of the CLR, whose job, after all, is to compile and interpret IL code in real time. Unsafe code, on the other hand, still operates in the managed environment but is not verified by the CLR for type safety or memory access before being interpreted. As a result, unsafe IL code may run faster than its "safe" counterpart, but it is *not* to be confused with native machine code.

Confusion arises because the Microsoft documentation frequently makes references to "unmanaged" code, without differentiating between native machine code and unsafe IL code. And if that weren't perplexing enough, VC.NET is capable of producing both unsafe IL code (when you use pointer manipulation that the CLR cannot verify) and native machine code (when you utilize libraries that compile to native code, such as the C-Runtime or Win32 API). A full discussion of VC.NET's code-generation nuances is beyond the scope of this CodeNote; but see ⊶CN⟩NET050001 for details. You can also find C# examples that use the `unsafe` keyword at ⊶CN⟩NET050002.

Proceed through this chapter with the understanding that you have three options to call native machine code from the managed environment: PInvoke to call Win32 DLLs, COM Interop to call COM components, and VC.NET that allows you to write native code and mix it in with managed code.

Topic: PInvoke and DllImport

In many respects, standard Win32 DLLs are still the backbone of the Windows operating system. A quick glance at the windows\system32 directory will reveal the hundreds of DLLs that are used to provide applications with services such as compression, encryption, and communication. For years, Visual Basic programmers have relied on such DLLs for functionality that transcends the language. The GetSystemDirectory() function in kernel32.dll for example, allows one to ascertain the full path of the windows\system32 directory, something that cannot be done directly in VB6.

Calling functions that reside in Win32 DLLs from managed applications is very similar to doing the same from previous versions of Visual Basic and is very straightforward. You simply declare the function prototype and the DLL in which the function is contained, and then call the function as if it resided directly in your source code. In the .NET Framework, you make such a declaration using the DllImport attribute, which can be found in the System.Runtime.InteropServices namespace (attributes are covered in Chapter 4). DllImport informs the CLR that the function exists in a DLL, and must be accessed using the CLR's Platform Invocation (PInvoke) services.

The C# code in Listing 5.1 calls the Sleep() function found in kernel32.dll, which delays program execution for a number of milliseconds. VB.NET and managed C++ versions can be found at ⊶NET050003.

```
using System;
using System.Runtime.InteropServices;

public class NativeExample
{
    // Use the DllImport attribute to declare the
    // Sleep function in kernel32.dll
    [DllImport("kernel32.dll")]
    public extern static void Sleep(uint msec);

    public static void Main()
```

```
{
  Console.Write("Delaying 1 second...");
  Sleep(1000);
  Console.WriteLine("done.");
}
}
```

Listing 5.1   Calling a Win32 DLL function from the managed environment

The extern keyword in the declaration of the Sleep() function informs the C# compiler that the method implementation will be found in the specified DLL. In Visual Basic, the declaration of an external DLL function is slightly different, as shown below.

```
Public Shared Function <DllImport("kernel32.dll")> _
  Sleep(byval msec as integer)
End Function
```

Whenever the Sleep() function is called by our program, the CLR will look in kernel32.dll for a function with the corresponding name, and call it if it finds one. If the function cannot be found, then a System .EntryPointNotFound exception will be thrown.

Calling Win32 functions from the managed environment frequently involves additional complexities such as error handling, variable marshaling, and aliasing. Such topics quickly plunge the developer into concepts such as Unicode strings, HRESULT error codes, and DLL entry points. Information on advanced PInvoke techniques can be found at NET050004.

HOW AND WHY

How Do I Handle Win32 DLL Functions That Use Callbacks?

Many functions in the Win32 API use callback functions. They accept a C-style function pointer (AddressOf in VisualBasic) and call this function to notify you that something has occurred. The CopyFileEx() function found in kernerl32.dll, for example, will copy a file and call your function repeatedly after a certain number of bytes have been copied.

To call a Win32 function that uses a callback from a .NET application, you must use a managed type of function pointer called a delegate. Delegates (covered in the Delegates section of Chapter 4) are similar to function pointers, except that they are type safe and allow the CLR to properly marshal data between the managed and unmanaged domains.

An example of using a delegate with the `CopyFileEx()` function can be found at ⌐CN̶NET050007.

A DLL I Have Written Exposes a Function I Want to Use in My Managed Program, but the CLR Keeps Telling Me That It Cannot Find It. What Am I Doing Wrong?

First, ensure that the DLL can be accessed by the CLR. The CLR will look for the DLL in the directories specified by the PATH environment variable and the application's directory. Assuming that the DLL can be found, use the DUMPBIN.EXE utility (see next question) to ensure that your function is being properly exported by the DLL. Many C++ compilers will obfuscate the exported function name through a phenomenon called name mangling. For a list of ways in which to rectify this, see ⌐CN̶NET050008.

Is There a Way to Determine the Functions That Are Exported by a Win32 DLL?

Microsoft provides a utility called DUMPBIN.EXE that allows you to do just that. Running

```
dumpbin.exe /exports MyDLL.dll
```

will list all the functions that are exported by MyDLL.dll. Some compilers also export functions by 16-bit "ordinal" numbers, which this utility also lists. The DllImport's Entrypoint option also allows functions to be declared by ordinal number. Examples of ordinal number decleration can be found at ⌐CN̶NET050009.

SUMMARY

The DllImport attribute found in the `System.Runtime.InteropServices` namespace allows managed applications to call functions that reside in Win32 DLLs. When a DLL function is called, the CLR must marshal its parameters and return values between the managed and unmanaged realms.

Topic: The COM Interop Service

The COM Interop service allows COM components to be called from the .NET environment. Like the PInvoke mechanism previously examined, COM Interop uses attributes to precisely describe the characteristics of the COM component being called. This helps the CLR construct a Runtime Callable Wrapper (RCW) that acts as a proxy between the COM component and your managed code. The RCW is responsible for invoking the COM component, marshaling parameters between the managed and unmanaged domains, and controlling the COM component's lifetime.

Many of the concepts discussed in this topic are very specific to COM. If you are unfamiliar with COM terminology (such as coclasses, IDL, interfaces, etc.), you can find a brief introduction at ⊶ᴺ⟩NET050023.

The TLBIMP utility

A utility provided with the .NET Framework called TLBIMP.EXE greatly simplifies COM integration, masking many of the conversion details from the developer. TLBIMP.EXE is a conversion tool; given a COM component it will generate an "interop" assembly that can be used in your managed programs. Your program uses the produced assembly as it would any other, completely unaware that the assembly has constructed an RCW behind the scenes, and that it is secretly communicating with a COM component.

The TLBIMP.EXE utility is designed to work with COM components that have type libraries. For those unfamiliar with type libraries, rest assured that VB-produced COM components contain them, as do the majority of components produced with popular frameworks such as ATL and even Visual J++. Calling the small minority of components without type libraries relies on the reflection technique examined in Chapter 4; an example can be found at ⊶ᴺ⟩NET050010.

Behind the scenes, TLBIMP.EXE is really utilizing the ConvertType LibToAssembly() method exposed by the System.Runtime.Interop-Services.TypeLibConverter class. You can, if you wish, use this class to programmatically convert COM type libraries into assemblies. In fact, this is what the VS.NET IDE implicitly does when a COM component is referenced from within a managed project.

Although Microsoft has tried to make the integration of COM components with managed applications as simple as possible, COM is an admittedly complex framework that can be used to create similarly complex components. Many of these complexities, such as aggregation, containment, custom marshaling, and multithreaded components, have been the sole privilege of C++ developers. While we will touch on techniques that C++ developers can use to integrate these more esoteric components throughout our example, a full discussion can be found at ⊶NET050011.

EXAMPLE

In this example we investigate how to call a C++ COM component called StockInfo from a managed application. Visual Basic users should also follow this example, as the migration of a VB component is identical. Portions of the COM and C# client code have been omitted for the sake of brevity, but the full source, as well as VB and managed C++ client code, is available at ⊶NET050012.

Assume that our component had one interface called IStockinfo, the IDL of which is given in Listing 5.2.

```
interface IStockInfo : IDispatch
{
  [ id(1), helpstring("method GetCurrentPrice") ]
  HRESULT GetCurrentPrice([in] BSTR bstrSymbol,
    [out] double *price);

  [ id(2), helpstring("method GetSymbolList") ]
  HRESULT GetSymbolList([out,retval] SAFEARRAY(BSTR) *pSymbol);
};
```

Listing 5.2   The IDL for the StockInfo COM component

Visual Basic abstracts the details of IDL from COM developers, but VB developers can assume that an IDL, similar to the one given in Listing 5.2, would have been generated by the language had they written an ActiveX class with the following methods:

```
Public Function GetCurrentPrice(ByVal Symbol As String)
As Double
  'Implementation
End Function

Public Function GetSymbolList(Symbol() As String)
  'Implementation
End Function
```

We will not provide the implementations for these methods (see NET050013), but for conceptual purposes assume that the Get-CurrentPrice() method returns the current price of the given stock symbol and GetSymbolList() returns an array of strings representing valid symbols.

Assuming that our DLL was called StockInfo.DLL, we could create an interop assembly using the TLBIMP utility as follows:

```
TLBIMP.EXE StockInfo.dll /out:StockInfoAsm.dll
```

If everything proceeds smoothly, TLBIMP will generate an assembly called StockInfoAsm.DLL. It is important to realize that this assembly is not a functional substitute for our COM component, as it doesn't contain executable code for either method. Rather, it contains the metadata that the CLR requires in order to create an RCW, which acts as a bridge between our managed program and the unmanaged COM component. We can examine the metadata of the interop assembly using the ILDASM tool introduced in the Metadata section in Chapter 3. Doing so brings up the following screen:

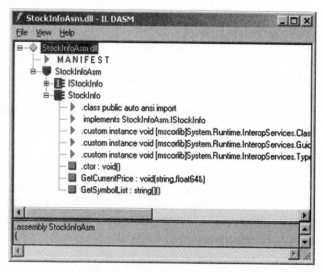

Figure 5.1   the StockInfoMeta Assembly

The Assembly's metadata reveals some interesting things. Note the presence of both the IStockInfo interface and the StockInfo class. These correspond to the COM component's interface and coclass. Although there is only one interface in our example, COM permits multiple interfaces per coclass, prompting developers to ask how these components are handled. See the online article at ⌀NET050018 for information on how to handle multi-interface COM components.

Turning our attention to the StockInfo class, we see that the GetSymbolList() method no longer returns an array of BSTRs (Visual Basic Strings), but rather an array of System.Strings. During the conversion process, the TLBIMP utility translated our unmanaged COM parameters into managed equivalents. This is especially nice for C++ developers, who no longer have to concern themselves with the deallocation of BSTRs (VB developers were abstracted from these details by the VB Runtime).

Another difference in the StockInfo class is that the new methods do not return HRESULTs, the COM-specific method by which errors are returned from components to their calling client. Visual Basic developers may be unfamiliar with HRESULTs, as the Visual Basic runtime abstracts the details of COM error checking. HRESULTS are used by VB behind the scenes, however, and failures communicated to the client via HRESULTs are what trips VB's "On Error Goto" mechanism. The COM Interop service offers a similar form of simplification by trapping errors from COM components and delivering them to your programs as exceptions of type System.Runtime.InteropServices.COM. A COM method that returned an HRESULT of E_OUTOFMEMORY, for example, would manifest itself as an OutOfMemoryException in your managed programs.

The one question that remains is the namespace used to access the assembly. From Figure 5.1 you will see that the StockInfo class resides in the StockInfoAsm namespace, which happens to have the same filename as our assembly (StockInfoAsm.DLL). This is no coincidence, as the namespace is derived directly from the interop assembly filename. Take care, then, in choosing the filename of the output DLL, as it will also serve as the namespace that clients use to access the COM component. If you fail to specify the assembly filename (that is, if you omitted the /out:StockInfoAsm.dll when executing TLBIMP), then the Runtime will derive both the namespace and the output filename from the IDL library name (the Project name in Visual Basic).

CALLING THE COM COMPONENT FROM C#

Listing 5.3 illustrates how the COM component, StockInfo, can be called from a C# application via the interop assembly that we generated with TLBIMP.EXE. VB.NET and managed C++ examples can be found at ⟨CN⟩NET050015.

```csharp
// Namespace reference to use the interop assembly.  If the
// assembly is private then it must in the same directory as
// the app. More on this in the assembly section in Chapter 3.
using StockInfoAsm;
using System.Runtime.InteropServices;
using System;


public class COMExample {

public static void Main()
{

// Create an instance of the StockInfo class contained
// in the StockInfoAsm assembly. Remember, this is not
// the COM object, but a 'proxy' to it.
StockInfo stockObj;
stockObj = new StockInfo();
double price = 0;


try {
  String[] symbols = stockObj.GetSymbolList();

  // print the prices of all available stocks
  for (int i = 0; i < symbols.GetLength(0); i++) {
    price = stockObj.GetCurrentPrice(symbols[i]);
    System.Console.Write("Price of {0}:", symbols[i]);
    System.Console.WriteLine("{0}",price.ToString());
  }

  // Try to get the price of an unavailable stock.  The
  // GetCurrentPrice method will return an HRESULT
  // error if this happens.
  price = stockObj.GetCurrentPrice("III");


}

// Catch any COM exceptions that the CLR propagates to
// us if our COM component returns an error.
catch (COMException e) {
```

```
        System.Console.WriteLine("COM error: {0}", e.Message);
    }
}
}
```

Listing 5.3   Calling the StockInfo component from the managed environment

Running this program produces the following output:

```
Price of AAA:2.56
Price of BBB:85.25
Price of CCC:45.6
Exiting program on COM error: Unspecified error
```

As can be seen from Listing 5.3, accessing a COM component from the .NET Framework is very straightforward once the interop assembly has been generated. In fact, the only way one could even tell that Listing 5.3 uses a COM component is that a COMException is being checked for. Other than that, the assembly is used like any assembly in the .NET Framework.

COM CALLABLE WRAPPERS

Just as COM components can masquerade as .NET assemblies, COM Interop permits the reverse to occur, allowing managed assemblies to masquerade as genuine COM components. To facilitate this, the COM Interop constructs a COM Callable Wrapper (CCW), which appears to unmanaged clients as a COM component. Like its RCW cousin, the CCW is really a proxy object that colludes with another entity across the managed/unmanaged boundary. The CCW also takes care of marshaling parameters between the two realms, as well as enforcing the security requirements of the managed assembly. Information on using CCWs in .NET can be found at °^{CN}⟩NET050016.

HOW AND WHY

I Ran TLBIMP.EXE on My COM Component, but the Conversion Failed. Where Do I Go from Here?

There is a small class of components that will not work successfully with TLBIMP. Conversion will fail if TLBIMP encounters difficulties in translating a method's parameters into managed equivalents. This occurs when your COM component is using a non-OLE data type, such as a custom defined structure. Such data types cannot be used in Visual Basic, and so (by implication) all VB COM components will convert without a problem. If you do have a C++ COM component that is utilizing such special types, you must write a custom "managed wrapper" in either C# or managed C++ in order to use it from the managed environment. An example of a managed wrapper that allows access to such a COM component can be found at ◦^{CN}NET050017.

What Is the Impact of COM Threading Models on My Managed Program?

Unlike the .NET Framework, COM can synchronize access to a component using apartments. Before a thread uses a COM component, it must inform COM as to the manner in which the component will be accessed. This allows COM to determine whether the component requires synchronization protection.

Although a complete discussion of COM threading models is beyond the scope of this CodeNote, you should be aware that all .NET threads will declare multithreaded apartment (MTA) affiliation by default. If the thread will be using single-threaded apartment (STA) components (such as those produced by VB6), this may adversely effect performance. You can explicitly declare a thread's concurrency model by using the ApartmentState field, found in the System.Threading namespace. An example of explicitly setting COM's threading model from the managed environment can be found at ◦^{CN}NET050018.

NATIVE CODE CAUTIONS

While many developers are likely to use the techniques in this chapter to call native code from the managed environment, caution must be taken when exercising this luxury. Recall that in the Core Concepts section of Chapter 4 we discovered that the CLR uses lightweight Appdomains to house .NET Applications.

Since a Win32 process houses multiple Appdomains (and thus multiple .NET Applications), if your native code does something illegal (such as referencing an invalid pointer) it will destroy the entire process, as well as any other .NET Applications running within it. This behavior is in contrast to misbehaving managed code, whereby the CLR would just shut down the individual Appdomain.

In addition to the dangers associated with executing native code, a performance hit is incurred any time native code is called from the managed environment. For this reason, it is a good idea to reduce the number of transitions from the managed to unmanaged realms. If native functions are to be used, you can reduce overhead by calling them a few times and performing many tasks within each individual call, as opposed to calling them many times and having each individual call perform a few tasks.

Many developers reason that one of the advantages of native code over managed code is the superior performance of the former. While this may seem reasonable given that native code is not subject to the CLR's scrutiny, be careful when exercising this assumption, as the .NET Runtime has been highly optimized. We have encountered a number of cases where the Runtime equals or outperforms its unmanaged equivalent (see ⌦NET050022). Even if native code performs slightly better, any speed gain can be easily nullified by the cost of transitioning to it in the first place.

SUMMARY

COM Interop allows managed applications to call COM components using interop assemblies. An interop assembly is produced from a COM type library using the TLBIMP utility, and once created it can be called from managed programs like any other assembly. Interop assemblies are used by the CLR to construct Runtime Callable Wrappers (RCW), which communicate with the actual COM component. The RCW takes care of marshaling parameters between the managed program and the unmanaged component.

COM Interop also allows managed components to be called by unmanaged clients, using COM Callable Wrappers (CCWs). CCWs give unmanaged clients the illusion they are communicating with COM components, although in fact they communicate with the .NET assembly. Like RCWs, CCWs take care of marshaling parameters between the managed and unmanaged worlds.

Chapter Summary

The .NET Framework offers developers three choices to call native code from the managed realm. Platform Invocation (PInvoke) services allow functions residing in Win32 DLLs to be called using the DllImport attribute. PInvoke exposes additional attributes to assist the CLR in marshaling data to such functions, particularly string types, which can be problematic. PInvoke also has facilities for handling functions that return error information in the form of HRESULTS.

Developers can use COM Interop to call COM components from managed applications, by generating interop assemblies from COM type libraries using the TLBIMP utility. The interop assembly can then be used as a genuine assembly in managed programs.

Chapter 6

—

ADO.NET

As relational databases become increasingly sophisticated, so too do the methods in which they are accessed. Vendors continually create new approaches to programmatically push and pull data from these robust storehouses, often to the frustration of developers, who are forever familiarizing themselves with the latest data access technologies. Over the years Microsoft has unveiled a number of database access technologies, each of which has been met with varying success: DAO, SQLDMO, RDO, OLEDB, and ADO. ADO.NET is a significant appendage to this lengthy list.

As its name suggests, ADO.NET is Microsoft's ActiveX Data Object (ADO) model for the .NET Framework. ADO.NET is not simply the migration of the popular ADO model to the managed environment but a completely new paradigm for data access and manipulation. ADO.NET, however, does not signal the end of ADO; developers can still use "traditional" ADO from the .NET environment using the COM Interop services discussed in Chapter 5. To call ADO from the managed environment, see the online instructions at ⟳NET06011.

Why ADO.NET?
The motivations behind ADO.NET can be best illustrated if we consider the shortcomings of its predecessor, ADO. Those unfamiliar with ADO should still be able to follow this instructional example. The following Visual Basic 6 ADO code connects to a remote SQL Server database called CodeNotes:

```
Dim mConnect As New ADODB.Connection
Dim mRecord As New ADODB.Recordset
Dim mCmd As New ADODB.Command

'Open Connection:
mConnect.ConnectionString = "driver={SQL
  Server};server=remoteServer;uid=sa;pwd=admin;
  database=CodeNotes"
mConnect.Open

'Obtain an ADO recordSet of the Stocks Table:
mCmd.CommandText = "Select * From CompanyTbl"
Set mCmd.ActiveConnection = mConnect
Set mRecord = mCmd.Execute

'Print all the StockIDs in the Stocks Table
Do While Not mRecord.EOF
  Print mRecord("StockSymb")
  mRecord.MoveNext
Loop

'Close connection since we are done reading data:
mConnect.Close
```

Listing 6.1   Accessing a remote database using ADO

We can make two observations about the preceding code. First, data access (reading the Stock Symbols) is done in the context of an open database connection. Second, the data retrieved is encapsulated as an ADO Recordset. If we wish to "send" this Recordset to another machine, we must do it using something called COM-marshaling, since ADO itself is exposed through COM.

Neither of these restrictions is problematic for the client/server model that ADO was originally designed for. Client/server applications are tightly coupled to their data sources, so continually having a database open is permissible. And, as the name suggests, client/server applications involve only two entities (a client application that requests data and a server application that provides it), both of whom, if they are using ADO, are fluent in COM.

While these stipulations are not problematic for the client/server model, they do present challenges for web-based scenarios. Web applications are loosely coupled, meaning they don't maintain continuous contact with their servers but communicate with them on a need-by-need basis. Since ADO prescribes that database manipulation must be performed in the context of an open connection, developers must ensure that these connections persist as a web application changes state (this is referred to as maintaining state). In addition to the problem of maintaining state, if we wish to share this data remotely with another entity on the Web, it must speak the underlying language of ADO, which is COM.

While it is true that ADO evolved to address some of these challenges—Remote Data Services (RDS), for example, introduced disconnected Recordsets—the ADO object model is still intrinsically connection-based, leaving room for improved Web integration.

Enter ADO.NET

Unlike ADO, ADO.NET is intended specifically for developing web applications. This is evident from its two major design principles:

1. Disconnected Datasets—In ADO.NET, almost all data manipulation is done outside the context of an open database connection. Data is read into an entity called a `Dataset` and the database is immediately closed. Operations (update/insert/delete) are performed against the `Dataset` as required. When the database is ready to be updated, it is reopened and data is imported from the `Dataset`.

2. Effortless Data Exchange with XML—Datasets can converse in the universal data format of the Web, namely XML. A `Dataset` can export its contents to XML, or import data in XML format. One is no longer restricted to exchanging data in proprietary COM format. This is especially important in the Internet's heterogeneous environment, where one may want to interoperate with non-Windows machines that lack support for COM.

ADO.NET's disconnected methodology leads to the natural division of its object model into two layers, the Managed Provider, which actually communicates with the database, and the disconnected Dataset, which performs the desired data manipulation. These entities communicate to each other using a Managed Provider's `DataAdapter` object, as illustrated in the ADO.NET model in Figure 6.1.

From Figure 6.1, we can see that the Dataset is the object that glues the ADO.NET Framework together, acting as a bridge between relational databases and the world of XML. The role of the Dataset as a mediator between these domains is significant, because it frees developers from having to represent their data in only one of these formats. With ADO.NET, one can take relational data and view it as hierarchical XML, so it can be utilized by XML parsers and XML technologies. At

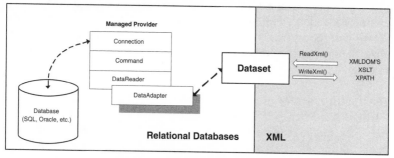

Figure 6.1   The ADO.NET Framework

the same time, one can take XML data and persist it to an SQL database. Examples in this chapter will demonstrate the portable data access inherent in the .NET Framework. The topic of .NET transactions, which falls more under the realm of general data access than of ADO.NET, will also be investigated.

CORE CONCEPTS

Schema

A schema is an XML document that describes the structures, constraints, and relationships of an XML data file. Since a schema is itself an XML document, it can be embedded in the XML data file that it depicts. Schemas are an important concept in this chapter, because of the intrinsic XML support in ADO.NET. The relationships expressed in an XML schema can be imported and enforced by a Dataset. Similarly, a Dataset can export its constraints and relationships to an XML schema.

Relational/Hierarchical Datasets

ADO.NET Datasets can access relational data that is stored in a database and XML data that is hierarchical. Relational data is compartmentalized into tables, columns, and rows, while its semantics (relationships, constraints, etc.), are stored separately from the data. Hierarchical data, like XML, is based on a "family tree" structure (parent/child/sibling elements). Because Datasets can read and write either of these formats, developers are no longer restricted to using one model to represent their data.

Serializable

An object is serializable if it can package itself as a sequence of bytes (its private member variables, associated data, etc.). Why would an object want to be serializable? Most often, so that it can be transported to a remote location where it can be recreated from those packaged bytes. As we will see in the Datasets section of this chapter, Datasets can serialize themselves as XML, making them easily transferable over the Internet.

The OLEDB Provider

OLEDB is a Microsoft COM-based standard that applications can utilize to exchange data with other applications. An OLEDB provider adheres to the OLEDB standard to expose its data store (usually a database) to clients (called OLEDB consumers). By offering a uniform interface to provide and consume data, clients are abstracted from the underlying particularities of the data store. In this sense, OLEDB is similar to the Open Database Connectivity Standard (ODBC) that preceded it. Unlike ODBC, which was a C-Style API, OLEDB uses COM, making it easily accessible from languages other than C and C++, such as Visual Basic.

With the advent of .NET, the OLEDB provider has evolved into what is now known as the Managed Provider. Like an OLEDB provider, a Managed Provider exposes a uniform set of classes that clients use to access data. Unlike OLEDB, Managed Providers speak in the language of the CLR (IL code), not COM. Managed Providers, however, do not make OLEDB providers obsolete. In fact, the .NET Framework includes a Managed Provider that "wraps" OLEDB providers, making them accessible from the managed environment. Managed Providers are the first topic of this chapter.

Topic: Managed Providers

Accessing a database using ADO.NET cannot proceed without a Managed Provider. Like an OLEDB provider or ODBC driver, a Managed Provider abstracts the specifics of its underlying database by exposing a common set of classes to applications. Most developers will only interact with a Managed Provider through these classes. The .NET Framework also ships with a Managed Provider SDK, for developers who want to write Managed Providers that expose a custom data store.

There are two Managed Providers that ship with the .NET Framework. The first is a dedicated optimized provider for SQL Server 2000 that is accessed through the System.Data.SqlClient namespace. The second, found in the System.Data.Oledb namespace, wraps existing OLEDB providers to make them accessible from the managed environment. Recall that an OLEDB provider is Microsoft's COM-based standard for data access. As of this writing, the following OLEDB providers ship with .NET:

1. SQLOLEDB: OLEDB provider for SQL Server 7.0 and above
2. MSDORA: OLEDB provider for Oracle
3. Microsoft.Jet.OLEDB.4.0: OLEDB provider for Jet (MS Access, etc.)

You may recognize that with ADO.NET it is possible to communicate with a SQL Server 2000 database in multiple ways. You can use either the dedicated SQL Provider or the Managed Provider that wraps the SQLOLEDB OLEDB provider. In general, a dedicated Managed Provider will outperform its wrapped OLEDB equivalent. This is because native OLEDB providers are invoked using the COM Interop services discussed in Chapter 5, whereas Managed Providers usually execute entirely within the managed realm.

A Managed Provider consists of four classes:

1. Connection: Used to establish a connection between the application and the data store. This class is very similar to the `Connection` object in ADO, as we will see in the upcoming example.
2. Command: Used to execute queries against the data store, whether stored procedures or standard SQL statements. Again, those familiar with ADO will find this analogous to the ADO Command object.
3. DataAdapter: As we will see in the next section, this class serves as the bridge between the connected Managed Provider and the disconnected Dataset. You will use this class to populate a Dataset and to update the database with a Dataset's modified contents.
4. DataReader: The DataReader is the only class where data access is performed in the context of an open database connection. A DataReader can only read records in forward manner. It is most often used to examine the results of a query, as we will see in the upcoming example.

In practice, you never use the four classes above directly. Instead, you will use Managed Provider classes, which inherit from these base classes. To open a connection using the SQL provider, for example, you would use the `SQLConnection` class. To do the same with the Managed Wrapper Provider, you would use the `OleDbConnection` class. The following example demonstrates the use of the SQL Server Managed Provider.

EXAMPLE

The Database
The examples in this chapter are centered around a simple SQL Server financial database called CodeNotes, depicted in the following diagram. We will use it to illustrate various ADO.NET features, such as constraints, XML integration, and schemas. Keep it in mind throughout this chapter, and refer back to it if necessary.

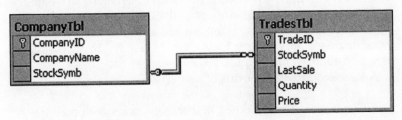

Figure 6.2   CodeNotes database

Our database consists of two tables, `CompanyTbl`, which stores Stock Symbols and their related company information, and `TradesTbl`, which stores the sales of a given stock, including the time and amount of the sale. You can create this SQL database either manually or by running the script found at ⊶NET060001.

The DataReader
This C# example will use the `DataReader` class to traverse through all the companies in the database. For this example, we will start with a partial listing and incrementally add lines of code until we have a working program. The full listing can be found online at ⊶NET060002.

The following block of code references the appropriate namespaces and connects to a database using the `SqlConnection` object. In this example, we are connecting to a local database called CodeNotes, with a user ID of "Example" and no password.

```
using System.Data;
using System.Data.SqlClient;

public class SimpleData {
  public static void Main()
```

```
{
  SqlConnection myConn = new SqlConnection(
    "user id=Example;password=;database=CodeNotes;" +
    "server=localhost");
  // More code here
}
}
```

Listing 6.2   SimpleData.cs framework and DB Connection

Having established a connection to the database, we now use the Command object to specify the SQL query we will use to retrieve data. Keep in mind that the following statement does *not* retrieve data from the database (the database hasn't been opened yet). Rather, it is used to specify the commands that will eventually execute against the database.

```
// Insert into Listing 5.2 after SQLConnection statement
SqlCommand myCommand =
  new SqlCommand("Select * from CompanyTbl",myConn);
```

To actually inspect data from the database, we open it using the SQLConnection object, and use SqlCommand class's ExecuteReader() method, which returns a DataReader object. The DataReader object can now be used to traverse through the records in the database.

```
// Insert into Listing 5.2 after the SQLCommand
statement
myConn.Open();
SqlDataReader myReader = myCommand.ExecuteReader();

while (myReader.Read()) {
  Console.WriteLine("{0} {1} {2}",
    myReader["CompanyID"], myReader["CompanyName"],
    myReader["StockSymb"]);
}
myConn.Close();
```

As with our ADO example at the beginning of this chapter (Listing 6.1), data is accessed in the context of an open connection. Note that you must call the DataReader's Read() method before you traverse through its records, in contrast to an ADO Recordset, which automatically points to the first record it contains.

The DataReader is the exception to ADO.NET's disconnected paradigm, and can be used when you want to quickly examine the results of a data query. With a DataReader, unlike in the Dataset object we will examine in the next section, records are not copied into memory; instead, reading each record requires hitting the database. For this reason, using a DataReader is appropriate for low memory situations, where the amount of returned records is large. Keep in mind, however, that a DataReader only allows you to view records—it does not allow you to modify them.

When compiling this program, don't forget to reference the System .Data.DLL assembly that is required to use the ADO.NET classes:

```
csc.exe /r:System.Data.dll SimpleData.cs
```

The line above produces the SimpleData.exe application, which, when run, produces the following output:

```
1 ACME SOFTWARE            AME
2 BABBLE CORP              BBC
3 ME INC                   MIC
```

In this example, we have used the SQL Managed Provider. Alternatively, we could have used the OLEDB Managed Provider in the System.Data.Oledb namespace. This provider would have used SQLOLEDB OLEDB provider to communicate with the SQL database. An example can be found at ⌁NET060003.

HOW AND WHY

How Do I Specify a Data Source Name (DSN) In My Connection String?
A popular way to connect to a database in the Windows environment is to use a Data Source Name. This is demonstrated in the following ADO code snippet:

```
Dim mConnect As New ADODB.Connection
mConnect.Open "DSN=MyDSN"
```

In order for this code to function correctly, a Data Source Name called MyDSN must be set up using the Windows ODBC Data Source Administrator. Among other things, this setup involves configuring the database's physical location and appropriate ODBC driver (SQL Server, Oracle, Access, etc.).

Recall that to communicate with a database using ADO.NET,

you need a Managed Provider. Unfortunately, neither of the Managed Providers that ship with ADO.NET (SQL Server and OLEDB Wrapper) allow you to specify a DSN when connecting to a database. At the time of this writing, you must download the ODBC.NET Data Provider from Microsoft in order to specify a DSN in your connection string. This package will install an assembly called System.Data.Odbc.DLL on your system. If you examine this assembly using ILDASM and look in the System.Data.Odbc namespace, you will find an ODBC Managed Provider that exposes the OdbcConnection, OdbcCommand, OdbcDataReader, and OdbcDataAdapter classes. You can now use the OdbcConnection class to specify a DSN in your connection string, much as in the preceding ADO code snippet. Example code, as well as instructions on how to download and install the ODBC.NET Data Provider, can be found at ☜NET060004.

How Do I Obtain Data Using a Stored Procedure Instead of an SQL Statement?

In the previous example we used a standard SQL statement to query data. To use a stored procedure you must set the SqlCommand's CommandType property to StoredProcedure. You must also denote the parameters the stored procedure will return using the SqlCommand's Parameters collection. A stored procedure example can be found at ☜NET060005.

SUMMARY

To access a database in ADO.NET you must use a Managed Provider. The .NET Framework ships with two managed providers: an optimized provider for SQL Server 2000 and a Managed Provider that wraps older COM-OLEDB providers, which were the preferred way to access databases before .NET. A Managed Provider contains four classes: Connection, Command, DataReader, and Dataset. The Connection and Command classes are used to connect to a database and execute queries against it. The DataReader class can be used to read the records of a database in a forward-only manner. A DataReader is the only class in the ADO.NET Framework that performs its operations against an open database connection. In the next section on Datasets, we will see how data can be manipulated in a disconnected fashion.

Topic: Datasets

ADO.NET is centered around the Dataset object. Using it together with the DataAdapter object of a Managed Provider, one can manipulate data outside the context of an open database connection.

Think of a DataAdapter as a messenger that ferries information from the database to the Dataset and vice versa. Much of this section will concern itself with the interplay between these two entities.

A DataAdapter is not the only way a Dataset can obtain data—XML is also a viable source and target. Datasets can read XML, and can make themselves available as XML to other clients. This is a significant feature; it means that developers can move data seamlessly between proprietary databases and universal XML. Examples that follow will explore the role of XML in the ADO.NET Framework.

It is tempting to think of a Dataset as an ADO Recordset, but this analogy has its limitations. While it is true that a Dataset can be used to access and modify data pulled from a database, it transcends the Recordset concept in a number of ways. Unlike a Recordset, a Dataset can house multiple tables and the relations between them. If the database has constraints (perhaps the combination of two fields must be unique), a Dataset can enforce this restriction. It is thus more accurate to think of a Dataset as a lightweight in-memory database (as opposed to a Recordset, which contains no relational information regarding the data it contains).

Because a Dataset can house multiple tables, it exposes a collection of DataTable classes. These in turn expose DataRow and DataColumn collections, representing the records and fields in the table(s). The various properties of the Dataset are illustrated in the following example.

EXAMPLE

In this example we demonstrate how the Dataset and DataAdapter classes can be used to add data to the CodeNotes database (see Figure 6.2). Specifically, we will add the Widget company (stock symbol WID) to the CompanyTbl table. When proceeding through this example, keep in mind that the CompanyID field is the table's primary key and must be unique for all records.

This example, in C#, will be presented in the same incremental fashion as the one in the last section. The full C# source is given at the end of this example as Listing 6.3, and can also be found at °^{CN}ϟNET060006.

As in the previous example, we begin by specifying the location of our database using the SqlConnection object and the data we wish to retrieve from it using the SqlCommand object:

```
using System.Data;
using System.Data.SqlClient;

public class SimpleData {
  public static void Main() {
    SqlConnection myConn = new SqlConnection(
      "user id=Example;password=;database=CodeNotes;" +
      "server=localhost");
    SqlCommand myCommand = new SqlCommand(
      "Select * from CompanyTbl",myConn);
  }
}
```

The next step is to declare a SqlDataAdapter object. When doing so, we give it the SqlCommand object we just created to provide it with the SQL statement used to retrieve data from the database.

```
SqlDataAdapter myDA = new SqlDataAdapter(myCommand);
```

We could have also given the DataAdapter the SQL statement directly and not used a Command object at all. The code below would be equivalent to the preceding two lines.

```
SqlDataAdapter myDA = new SqlDataAdapter(
  "Select * from CompanyTbl",myConn);
```

Remember, the database has not been opened yet. The SQL statement will be used when we use the SqlDataAdapter's Fill() method to populate a Dataset with data. We do that right now:

```
DataSet myDS = new DataSet();
myDA.Fill(myDS, "Companies");
```

When it is executed, the DataAdapter's Fill() method does the following: it opens the database, executes the SQL statement, populates the Dataset with the results, and closes the database connection. The second parameter in the Fill() method specifies that data be stored in the Dataset's Companies table. This may seem confusing, given that we pulled the data from the database's CompanyTbl table. Remember that a Dataset is in-memory data holder—the source of its data is irrelevant, be it SQL Server, Oracle, or, as we will see, XML. You determine the names of its tables, not the database that populates it. It may help to think of this operation as the transfer of data from the database's CompanyTbl table to the Dataset's Companies table.

Each table in a Dataset (remember that a Dataset can store more than one) exposes Column and Row collections, which represent the fields and records in the table. To obtain the names of all the fields in the Companies table, we iterate through the Columns collection like so:

```
foreach (DataColumn column in
myDS.Tables["Companies"].Columns) {
  Console.WriteLine("{0}",column.Caption);
}
```

This code would print out the following:

```
CompanyID
CompanyName
StockSymb
```

The Rows collection of a table is also how we add, modify, and delete records in a table. The following code adds the Widget company to the Companies Table:

```
DataRow myRow = myDS.Tables["Companies"].NewRow();
myRow["CompanyName"] = "Widget Corp.";
myRow["StockSymb"] = "WID";
myDS.Tables["Companies"].Rows.Add(myRow);
```

Notice that we specified the row's field by name: myRow-["StockSymb"]. As in ADO, it is also permissible to reference the rows by ordinal number: myRow[0], myRow[1], etc. It is important to realize that the new record has *not* been added to the underlying database, only to the in-memory table of the Dataset. To update the database we have to use our bridge to the relational world—the DataAdapter.

Before we update the database (using the DataAdapter's Update() method), we need to consider how this operation is performed. Here, the DataAdapter must perform the reverse operation of the Fill() method: it must transfer the data from the Dataset's Companies table to the database's CompanyTbl table.

Remember that a Dataset's table is entirely within our jurisdiction.

We could have added and removed fields from it, or (as we will see) established relationships with other tables. The DataAdapter has no idea how to map our possibly modified table to the one in the underlying database. We need to help it out, and we can do so using a DataAdapter's `InsertCommand`, `UpdateCommand`, and `DeleteCommand` properties. These properties accept SQL statements that a DataAdapter executes when it has to insert, update, and delete rows in the database. It is important to realize that these three properties are specific to DataAdapters whose underlying data store is SQL-specific. If you were using a DataAdapter for a non-SQL entity, it would have to expose some other mechanism to update the underlying data store.

Providing an SqlDataAdapter object with three SQL statements every time we wish to update a database is tedious. If our operation is simple enough (if we will only be modifying one table), the `SqlCommandBuilder` class can automate the process for us:

```
// Note myDA is the SqlDataAdapter
SqlCommandBuilder mBuild = new SqlCommandBuilder(myDA);
```

Including the line above in our source populates the DataAdapter with the appropriate `InsertCommand`, `UpdateCommand`, and `DeleteCommand` properties. If our update operation was more complex (if we wanted to update multiple tables at once), we would have to manually provide these statements. An example that uses the manual approach can be found at ⦿^{CN}NET060007. With the `SqlCommandBuilder` statement in place, we can update the underlying database.

```
myDA.Update(myDS,"Companies");
```

Note that when specifying the table to update you use the Dataset's table name, not the database's one. The entire source for the Dataset update operation is recreated in Listing 6.3:

```
// Note myDA is the SqlDataAdapter
using System.Data;
using System.Data.SqlClient;

public class SimpleData
{
public static void Main()
{
  SqlConnection myConn = new SqlConnection(
    "user id=sa;password=;database=CodeNotes;server=PooBong");
```

```
SqlCommand myCommand = new SqlCommand(
  "Select * from CompanyTbl",myConn);
SqlDataAdapter myDA = new SqlDataAdapter(myCommand);
DataSet myDS = new DataSet();
myDA.Fill(myDS, "Companies");

DataRow myRow = myDS.Tables["Companies"].NewRow();
myRow["CompanyName"] = "WidgetCorp.";
myRow["StockSymb"] = "WI1";
myDS.Tables["Companies"].Rows.Add(myRow);

// Note myDA is the SqlDataAdapter
SqlCommandBuilder mBuild = new SqlCommandBuilder(myDA);
myDA.Update(myDS,"Companies");
}
}
```

Listing 6.3   Adding a company to the CodeNotes database

Compile and run the program (don't forget to reference System.Data .DLL), and the Widget company will be added to the CompanyTbl table—something you can confirm using the SimpleData.exe application we developed in the previous section on Managed Providers.

You may have noticed that we did not specify a CompanyID when adding the Widget company to the database. We got away with this because, in addition to being the primary key of the table, the CompanyID field was configured to AutoIncrement in the SQL Server database. When SQL Server received our request to add the new row, it examined the CompanyID field, and seeing that it was empty, assigned it a unique value based on those records already in the table.

We cannot always rely on the underlying database for this type of protection. It is possible for a field to be unique but not AutoIncremented so that the database rejects empty values. It would be more rigorous if we could enforce this uniqueness programmatically. To do this, we need to know that CompanyID is the table's primary key—that is, we need the database's schema. We get this information using the DataAdapter's FillSchema() method:

```
myDA.FillSchema(myDS,SchemaType.Mapped,"Company");
```

You must run the FillSchema() method before you retrieve the table's data using Fill(). As a result of the FillSchema() operation, the Dataset's column that represents the CompanyID field has its

Unique and AutoIncrement properties set to true. Unfortunately, the FillSchema() method does not set the column's AutoSeed property. So, although our Dataset is now aware that the CompanyID column is unique and must increment itself automatically, it has no idea where the numbering should start. To combat this shortcoming, you must explicitly set the AutoSeed property by iterating through all the returned records and noting the highest number in the CompanyID field. Code that demonstrates this can be found at ⟨CN⟩NET060008.

From this example, it should be apparent that a Dataset is more than a representation of data, but rather a powerful in-memory relational data store. Its versatility goes beyond what we have demonstrated here. You can, for example, add your own constraints to one of its tables, or establish relationships between tables using foreign keys. Examples that demonstrate these features can be found at ⟨CN⟩NET060009. Lastly, remember that the manipulation we performed (adding a new record) was done outside the context of a database connection. The database was only opened when we retrieved data using the Fill() method and updated it using Update().

XML SUPPORT

The previous example illustrated how to transfer data between a Dataset and a relational database. Here, we consider the other source and recipient of a Dataset's contents: XML. In addition to the capabilities we have already seen, a Dataset can serve as an intermediary between these two mediums. Any data it obtains from a relational database can be manipulated and saved as XML, and any data that is retrieved as XML can be stored in a database.

Before we examine how a Dataset can read and write XML, it is worth noting that a Dataset itself is serialized in XML. Why is this significant? Recall our discussion on ADO earlier, where we discovered that to transport an ADO Recordset to a remote location we had to use a process called COM-marshaling. This prescribed that the remote machine be fluent in COM. Serialization in XML removes this limitation, allowing us to send a Dataset to any remote machine in the ubiquitous language of the Web. (This is something we will revisit in the SOAP section of Chapter 8.) Network gurus will also note that XML can be sent over the unrestrictive HTTP protocol, whereas COM-marshaling uses other protocols that can be problematic when firewalls exist between the two machines.

To save a Dataset's contents to XML, you use its WriteXml() method.

We could save the contents of the Companies table from the previous example to a file called Company.XML as follows:

```
myDS.WriteXml("Company.XML",XmlWriteMode.WriteSchema);
```

You may be wondering what the second parameter, XmlWriteMode .WriteSchema, does. Remember that a Dataset contains both data and the semantics to use it (constraints, relationships, etc.). The second parameter informs WriteXML() to include the Dataset's relational schema when writing the XML file. Alternatively, we can specify that the schema be saved to a separate file:

```
myDS.WriteXml("Company.Xml",XmlWriteMode.IgnoreSchema);
myDS.WriteXmlSchema("CompanySchema.Xsd");
```

XSD is a standard for writing schemas, hence the .XSD extension on the schema file. If you examine this schema (CompanySchema.Xsd) using a text editor, you will see something like the file depicted in Listing 6.4.

```xml
<?xml version="1.0" standalone="yes"?>
<xsd:schema id="NewDataSet" targetNamespace="" xmlns=""
xmlns:xsd="http://www.w3.org/2001/XMLSchema"
xmlns:msdata="urn:schemas-microsoft-com:xml-msdata">
  <xsd:element name="NewDataSet"
msdata:IsDataSet="true">
    <xsd:complexType>
      <xsd:choice maxOccurs="unbounded">
        <xsd:element name="Companies">
          <xsd:complexType>
            <xsd:sequence>
              <xsd:element name="CompanyID"
msdata:DefaultValue="NULL" type="xsd:int" minOccurs="0"
msdata:Ordinal="0" />
              <xsd:element name="CompanyName"
msdata:DefaultValue="NULL" type="xsd:string"
minOccurs="0" msdata:Ordinal="1" />
              <xsd:element name="StockSymb"
msdata:DefaultValue="NULL" type="xsd:string"
minOccurs="0" msdata:Ordinal="2" />
            </xsd:sequence>
          </xsd:complexType>
        </xsd:element>
      </xsd:choice>
```

```
     </xsd:complexType>
     <xsd:unique name="Constraint1">
       <xsd:field xpath="CompanyID"/>
     </xsd:unique>
   </xsd:element>
</xsd:schema>
```

Listing 6.4   The Dataset's structure exported to an XML schema file

As can be seen, the XML schema contains the fields in the Dataset, as well as the unique constraint on the `CompanyID` field. Most often, you will want to save a schema directly with the XML file. The ability to do this is important, because the XML file now fully describes the data it contains. If another entity reads it, it can read the schema and enforce its constraints and rules. Such an entity might be a database capable of reading XML, like SQL Server, or a Document Object Model (DOM), reader like Microsoft's XmlDocument class found in the `System.XML` namespace. Another potential recipient of XML could be . . . another Dataset.

Reading XML into a Dataset is almost as simple as writing it:

```
myDS.ReadXml("Company.Xml",XmlReadMode.Fragment);
```

The counterintuitively named `XmlReadMode.Fragment` parameter tells `ReadXml()` that the schema is contained within the XML file. It will read the schema and construct the corresponding constraints and relationships in the Dataset. You cannot, however, always ensure that an XML file will contain a schema. In such cases you must use the `XmlReadMode.Auto` and `XmlReadMode.InferSchema` parameters, the former when you are unsure of a schema's presence in the XML file, the latter when you are certain it is absent.

What happens if `ReadXml()` encounters an XML file without a schema? In this case, it will try to *infer* a schema based on the data in the XML file. This heuristic approach is interesting and complex, but beyond the scope of this CodeNote. For details, see ^{CN}NET060010.

Before we finish with this topic, we have to mention that in addition to reading and writing files, the `ReadXML()` and `WriteXML()` methods can also read and write to streams, strings, and even the `XmlReader` and `XmlWriter` classes found in `System.Xml` namespaces. See ^{CN}NET060011 for additional examples.

One last feature of ADO.NET that we must mention is *typed* Datasets. To access Recordset fields in traditional ADO, developers used statements such as `myRS["SomeField"] = "hello"`. With ADO.NET typed Datasets, you can write the more intuitive and compiler-friendly `myRS.SomeField` = `"hello"`. The difference between these two statements is that the second one can be type-checked by the compiler, whereas the first one cannot. Information on typed ADO.NET Datasets can be found at ⟶NET06011.

HOW AND WHY

How Does a DataAdapter Determine the Rows That Have Been Modified in a Dataset?

In order to `Update()` its underlying database, a DataAdapter must know those rows that have been modified in the Dataset. To facilitate this, the Dataset maintains four copies of the rows in its tables: Default/Original/Current/Proposed. The two important ones are Original and Current, respectively representing a row's value when the Dataset was first created and its current value, if it has changed. The DataAdapter compares these two values to determine which rows should be updated.

Because a Dataset keeps track of changing row values, it exposes a rich event model whereby one can accept or reject changes to its underlying data. This involves using the `BeginEdit()`, `EndEdit()`, `AcceptChanges()`, and `RejectChanges()` methods. Details can be found at ⟶NET060010.

SUMMARY

Datasets are in-memory data stores that manipulate data outside the context of database connections. Like a database, a Dataset can house multiple tables, and the relationships and constraints on the data within those tables. A Dataset interacts with a database using a Managed Provider's DataAdapter class, using `Fill()` to read data and `Update()` to write it. Datasets can also read and write data in XML and can import/export their schemas as XML schemas. This capability allows developers to seamlessly expose a Dataset's contents to XML-capable entities such as XML parsers, XSLT, and so on.

Topic: Transactions

It is often desirable to have database access proceed in the context of a transaction. In the context of a transaction, operations are *atomic,* meaning they either all succeed or are not performed at all. This capability can sometimes be provided by the database itself. If, for example, you INSERT several rows into a database table in the context of a transaction and one of the insertions fail, the database can undo all the previous successful INSERTs.

Scenarios may arise where you want explicit control over those operations that are atomic. Consider the following code that might execute when ten customers have purchased an item for twenty dollars:

```
cmd1.CreditAccounts(TenCustomerAccounts, 20.00);
cmd2.DebitAccounts(SomeCompany,200.00);
```

While the underlying database(s) may assure us that each individual operation is atomic (either all customer accounts are credited or they are not), the code as it exists does not guarantee collective atomicity. It is possible that after crediting each customer account, the system might crash and the company account not be debited. This unfortunate predicament is sure to confuse the company's accountant.

To combat this situation, the .NET Framework allows us to place operations within a transaction, so they collectively either succeed or fail. As the following examples illustrate, we can do this manually using the Connection class of a Managed Provider, or automatically using the Transaction attribute found in the Runtime classes.

EXAMPLE: MANUAL TRANSACTIONS

The Connection class of a Managed Provider exposes the Begin Transaction(), CommitTransaction(), and RollbackTransaction() methods that can be used to make a group of operations atomic. Consider the following code fragment:

```
try {
// myName is a string, required to name the transaction
  myConn.BeginTransaction();
  cmd1.CreditAccounts(TenCustomerAccounts, 20.00);
  cmd2.DebitAccounts(SomeCompany,200.00);
  myConn.CommitTransaction();
} catch (Exception e) {
  Console.WriteLine("Error: Transaction Aborted.");
  myConn.RollbackTransaction();
}
```

Listing 6.5   Manual .NET Transactions

Before both account operations execute, they are placed within a transaction. If both operations succeed, the transaction is committed (changes are made permanent). If an exception occurs during either operation, then both operations are undone using RollbackTransaction(). Manual transactions can only be used in the context of an open database connection, so they cannot be used with connectionless Datasets.

EXAMPLE: AUTOMATIC TRANSACTIONS

Using the Transaction attribute (attributes are covered in Chapter 4), you can specify that all the methods of a class be performed in the context of a transaction. If a method proceeds without an exception being generated, the transaction commits. If not, the transaction aborts.

To use an automatic transaction, apply the Transaction attribute found in the System.EnterpriseServices namespace to a class that must inherit from System.ServicesComponent. Its methods are then marked with the AutoComplete attribute, also found in the System .EnterpriseServices namespace. This is demonstrated in the code below.

```
using Microsoft.EnterpriseServices;

[Transaction]
public class myAccountClass : ServicesComponent
{
  [AutoComplete]
  public void TransferMoney()
  {
    cmd1.CreditAccounts(TenCustomerAccounts, 20.00);
    cmd2.DebitAccounts(SomeCompany,200.00);
  }
}
```

As a result of including the AutoComplete and Transaction attributes, TransferMoney() is performed in the context of a transaction (created by the CLR). Remember, the outcome of the transaction is determined based on the behavior of the method; if the method completes normally, the transaction commits. If an exception is raised, the transaction aborts.

You can explicitly inform the CLR of a transaction's outcome using the SetComplete() and SetAbort() methods of the ContextUtil class. SetComplete() indicates to the CLR that the transaction should commit, while SetAbort() indicates that the transaction should abort. It is important to realize that the CLR does not decide on the result of the transaction until the method terminates. The rule of thumb, therefore, is that the last call to either SetComplete() or SetAbort() determines the transaction's outcome. Thus, if a method encounters a problem, it can indicate that, for the time being, the transaction should abort. If the problem is rectified at some later point (in the same method), you can reverse the transaction's outcome by calling SetComplete(). The following code demonstrates SetComplete() and SetAbort():

```
Using Microsoft.ComService; // Needed for ContextUtil
...
public void TransferMoney() {
  cmd2.DebitAccounts(SomeCompany,200.00);
  // some problem in our code, so indicate
  // that we can't commit:
  ContextUtil.SetAbort();
  // We rectify the problem, so indicate we can
  // commit now:
  ContextUtil.SetComplete();
  // SetComplete() was called last, so transaction
  // commits.
}
```

The SetComplete() and SetAbort() methods first surfaced in Microsoft Transaction Server (MTS), and then later in MTS's Windows 2000 incarnation, COM+. They continue to exist in the managed environment, in what is more than just a coincidental naming scheme. When an object that uses the Transaction attribute is instantiated, the CLR creates a transaction-enabled COM+ component behind the scenes to house it. You can influence the transaction properties of the created COM+ component by using additional parameters in the Transaction attribute. For details, see ⟲NET060012.

Our realization that the CLR can cooperate with COM+ is important, because it allows us to take advantage of additional COM+ services from the managed environment. Look in the System.EnterpriseServices namespace and you will find support for object pooling, queued components, and role-based security. Note that any assembly that uses COM+ services must be signed with a private key so as to give it a strong name (see the Shared Assemblies section in Chapter 3 for details on strong naming).

INTERNAL VS. EXTERNAL TRANSACTIONS

At the beginning of this section we said that all the operations enclosed within a transaction were collectively atomic. It is vital that we revisit this assumption. If you modify two databases within a transaction and it aborts, do both databases rollback? If so, who coordinates their efforts? Clearly, if a transaction is to be distributed, there must be some entity that oversees it and alerts participating databases of its outcome. In the Windows environment, this entity is called the Distributed Transaction Coordinator (DTC).

The DTC's role in a transaction gives rise to two transaction types. Internal transactions run against one database and the DTC knows nothing about them. External transactions run under the auspices of the DTC and can span multiple databases. In order for a database to participate in an external transaction, it must be able to talk to the DTC—it must be "DTC-aware."

Consider the `BeginTransaction()` and `CommitTransaction()` methods that enable you to manually regulate transactions. Look back at the manual transaction example (Listing 6.5) and you will see that these methods are used in the context of a connection to a Managed Provider. These are internal transactions that are not enlisted with the DTC, so they cannot involve other databases. The transaction is only valid against the database the Managed Provider is talking to.

COM+ transactions, however, are external. Databases that are accessed from within such a transaction register themselves with the DTC (assuming they are DTC-aware). When the transaction completes, the DTC informs each database of the transaction's outcome so that it can act accordingly (i.e., either commit or undo changes).

Any database you access through an ADO.NET Managed Provider (SQL Server, Oracle) is DTC-aware and can participate in an external transaction. Nor are you limited to ADO.NET; if you access a DTC-aware database through ADO or RDO, it too can participate in the transaction.

Using the `Transaction` and `AutoComplete` attributes, then, you can place both ADO and ADO.NET code in the same method and have them unanimously commit or abort. If the method completes, the DTC will instruct both underlying databases to commit. If an exception is raised, both databases will be told to undo any changes they've made. This assumes that the ADO and ADO.NET code are communicating with different databases; it is possible that the same database is being used. For examples of intermixing these two frameworks within a single transaction, see ℂℕ NET060014.

HOW AND WHY

Do Multiple Methods Marked with the AutoComplete Attribute Share the Same Transaction?

Consider what occurs when you use the AutoComplete attribute: a method's code executes within a transaction. If it completes without error, the transaction is committed. If an exception is raised, the transaction is aborted. In either case, the transaction is completed when the method exits. If you call another method marked with the AutoComplete attribute (or even the same method again), the CLR will create a new transaction before the method executes.

Thus, each call to a method marked with AutoComplete results in a new transaction being created and destroyed. The only way to share a single transaction between multiple methods, or multiple calls to the same method, is to forgo use of the AutoComplete attribute and use the SetComplete() and SetAbort() methods of the ContextUtil class. An example can be found at ☞NET060015.

SUMMARY

Database operations are often performed in the context of a transaction. A transaction makes a group of operations atomic, meaning their results persist only if every operation is successful. The Connection class of a Managed Provider exposes the BeginTransaction(), CommitTransaction(), and RollbackTransaction() methods that allow one to manually create a transaction for a group of operations. Transactions of this type are internal, meaning only those operations that execute against the Managed Provider's underlying database are atomic.

The Transaction and AutoComplete attributes can be applied to a class and its methods, respectively, which automatically makes the methods of the class transactional. If a method proceeds to completion, the transaction commits. If an exception is raised, the transaction aborts. Transactions of this type are external, meaning they can span multiple databases. To participate in an external transaction, a database must be DTC-aware. The Managed Providers that ship with ADO.NET all communicate with DTC-aware databases.

Chapter Summary

ADO.NET is the data access model for the managed environment. ADO.NET is based upon the disconnected paradigm, which means that data manipulation is performed outside the context of an open database connection.

To communicate with a database in ADO.NET you need a Managed Provider, which abstracts an underlying database by providing four uniform classes: Connection, Command, DataAdapter, and DataReader, of which the two most significant are Connection and DataAdapter. As its name suggests, the Connection class is used to establish a connection with the database, while the DataAdapter class acts as a bridge between the database and the most important class in the ADO.NET Framework, the Dataset.

A Dataset is an in-memory data store that can house multiple tables, and the relationships and constraints on the data within those tables. In ADO.NET you populate a Dataset using a DataAdapter's Fill() method, manipulate the Dataset's contents, and then sink changes back to the database using the DataAdapter's Update() method. Datasets can also communicate with the world of XML, exporting their data/relationships to XML data/schema files and vice versa. This is a significant feature of ADO.NET, as it means that developers can easily move data between relational databases and hierarchical XML.

The .NET Runtime also allows one to place database operations within a transaction, which makes those operations atomic—either they all succeed or they are not performed at all. Transactions can be either manual, using the Connection class of a Managed Provider, or automatic, using the Transaction and AutoComplete attributes found in the System.EnterpriseServices namespace. Manual transactions must be explicitly committed or aborted using a Connection class's BeginTransaction(), CommitTransaction(), RollbackTransaction() methods. Methods marked with the AutoComplete attribute are automatically housed within a transaction, which either commits, if the method completes without failure, or aborts, if the method raises an exception.

Chapter 7

—

WINDOWS FORMS

OVERVIEW

In this chapter we examine Windows Forms, a collection of classes that wrap the Windows API and are used to create Graphical User Interfaces (GUIs) for the managed environment. These classes can be called in a programmatic manner (similar to C or MFC development) or can be utilized by the Windows Form Designer (WFD) of the VS.NET IDE, which calls them behind the scenes whenever you design a screen graphically, as you do in Visual Basic 6. Because the Windows Forms classes exist as managed code, they can be inherited across languages. The Visual Inheritance topic in this chapter, for example, will demonstrate how one can develop a GUI in Visual Basic and extend it in C#.

Windows Forms is not to be confused with Web Forms, covered in Chapter 8, which is the new user interface framework for developing web applications. There are remarkable similarities between these two frameworks, however, and developers familiar with one can easily transition to the other.

Visual Basic 6 developers will be especially interested in Windows Forms, since it is now the underlying engine behind VB.NET Form Design. The changes from Visual Basic 6 to Windows Forms are significant—many of the intrinsic controls in VB6 such as buttons, textboxes, and labels have changed considerably and now exist in the Windows Forms classes. This chapter will discuss some of these changes, as well as some of the completely new features in the Windows Forms framework.

Another new technology for designing desktop applications is GDI+, the managed version of the Windows Graphics Device Interface (GDI) used to draw graphics on the video display. GDI+ is a powerful graphics package that can be used for drawing shapes, filling surfaces with gradients and textures, and loading and manipulating images. Information on GDI+ and source examples can be found at ⟳NET070011.

GUI REVIEW AND THE WINDOWS FORMS CLASSES

To introduce Windows Forms, let's ask ourselves how (prior to .NET) we would create the following simple Windows application that closes itself when its button is pressed.

Figure 7.1   Simple application

One option would be to write it in C and use the Windows API directly. If we decided to take this route, we would use the CreateWindows() API function to create the form and button, associate the form with a message pump (similar to DoEvents in VB), process the application's incoming messages, and write application termination code to respond to the button's click event, all the while ensuring that our C code set up the function parameters properly and accounted for the numerous idiosyncrasies in the Windows API.

As you have probably guessed, it is unlikely that we would employ this arduous approach. The eighty-some-odd lines of aforementioned C code could be replaced with the following three lines in Visual Basic (after we had drawn a button on our resized form in the VB6 environment):

```
Private Sub Command1_Click()
  Unload Me 'They pressed the button -- unload the form.
End Sub
```

Listing 7.1   Simple VB6 code.

How did we go from eighty lines of C to only three lines in Visual Basic? The answer is the VB Forms Engine, which, behind the scenes, performs all of the aforementioned grunt work for us. These operations are buried somewhere in the VB Runtime but are implicitly invoked every time a Visual Basic application executes. Because of this, VB developers are abstracted from the Windows API that is implicitly called by their programs. While this is usually a blessing, it can be limiting when one wants finer control over one's applications. It would be nice if VB exposed its underlying plumbing so we could, if we wanted, modify and build on it—that is, it would be nice if the VB Forms Engine revealed the API calls it was making. .NET's replacement for the VB Forms Engine, the Windows Form Designer, does just that. The only difference is that it makes and reveals not Windows API calls but managed classes found in the System.Windows.Forms namespace.

Creating applications using the WFD is much like in previous versions of Visual Basic: you draw your application's graphical elements on a form and then write the event handlers behind them. When you draw a button or change its caption or change its size, the WFD translates your manipulations into VB or C# code that calls the Windows Forms classes. This code is placed into a special region of the code listing, marked with #region and #endregion tags (as seen in the upcoming example).

At the heart of the Windows Forms classes lies the Control class. Any managed component that has a GUI element must derive from this class, which handles user input and operating system notifications such as repaint requests. Because of this, the Control class is at the top of the component hierarchy depicted in Figure 7.2.

As can be seen in Figure 7.2, other controls in the Windows Forms framework extend the basic functionality of the Control class. ScrollableControl adds scrolling ability to a control, while Container Control gives a control the ability to house other controls by providing focusing and tabbing functionality. Two descendents of this class, UserControl and Form, are the ones you will interact with most often. The Form class is equivalent to a form in Visual Basic and is used to create Window Screens and Dialog boxes in the managed environment, while the UserControl class can be used to create your own custom managed controls.

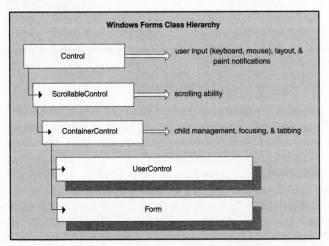

Figure 7.2   The Windows Forms class hierarchy

When you create a form (let's call it MyForm) in VB.NET, the WFD produces a corresponding MyForm class that inherits from the Form class in Figure 7.2. Likewise, many of the intrinsic controls in VB6 are now found in the Windows.Forms namespace. If you examine the System.Windows .Forms.DLL assembly using ILDASM and look in the Windows.Forms namespace, you will find Button, Label, and Textbox classes, all of which are used when the corresponding control is used in VB.NET.

The biggest challenge for VB developers will be to familiarize themselves with the way these classes have changed from their intrinsic VB6 counterparts. You cannot, for example, Unload a form as we did with the VB 6 code in Listing 7.1. As we will see shortly, you must use the form's Close() method. Numerous other syntax changes are discussed in the online article found at ⚙NET070003.

If you remember that an assembly contains language-neutral IL code, you'll recognize that the Windows Forms classes are accessible in languages other than VB. To graphically construct applications as in VB6, however, you need a tool such as the WFD to translate your graphical manipulations into code. As of this writing, the WFD can only generate code in VB.NET and C#. So if you wish to call the Windows Forms classes using other languages, such as managed C++, you must do so programmatically, without the benefit of an intuitive design environment. This means that you must instantiate and configure the Windows Forms classes manually, much like when using MFC or the Windows API.

From a conceptual perspective, you can think of the Windows Forms Designer as a powerful wizard that constantly translates your pictorial constructions into either VB.NET or C# code.

EXAMPLE

Up to this point, we have compiled all of our programs from the command line. In this chapter, we will utilize the VS.NET IDE so that we can use the Windows Form Designer. The VS.NET IDE is an amalgamation of the Visual Studio 6 and VB6 suites—gone are the days of separate development environments for Visual Basic and C++. We will write a simple GUI using the Windows Form Designer, and have the WFD produce VB.NET code for us behind the scenes. We will then create an identical GUI using the WFD, except that we will get it to produce C# code for us the second time around.

After starting VS.NET, go to the File menu and select New and then Project. This will bring up the screen in Figure 7.3. (The very first time you bring up VS.NET, it will ask you to choose a keyboard scheme and Windows layout based on the previous environment you are coming from, VB or Visual Studio. Choose the one you are most comfortable with.)

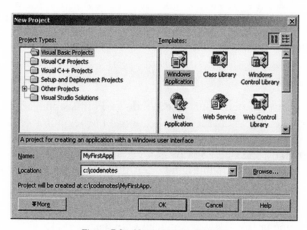

Figure 7.3   New project in VS.NET

After bringing up this screen, select Visual Basic Projects under Project Types, and Windows Application under Template. Give your project a name (we called ours MyFirstApp), specify the directory in which it will be contained, and click OK. VS.NET will create a Visual Basic Project for you with an empty form. The environment looks very much like previous versions of Visual Basic: take a moment to explore it.

Drag a button from the toolbox onto your form and resize it so that you have something like the following:

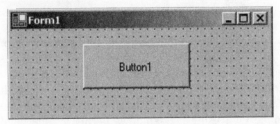

Figure 7.4   First Visual Basic application

Double-click Button1 and insert the line Me.Close() so that you have the following code in front of you:

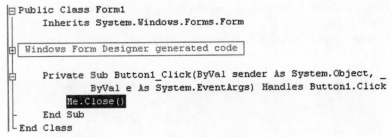

Figure 7.5   Project code

You have just written your first Windows Forms application, which functions like the hypothetical application at the beginning of this chapter, automatically closing itself when its button is pressed. You can run the program by pressing F5 or by going to the Debug menu and clicking Start. Note that the code in Figure 7.5 is different from the VB6 code in Listing 7.1 in five respects:

1. The line Unload Me was replaced with Me.Close().
2. The method associated with the button's click event (Button1_Click) is more complex than its VB6 equivalent. As we learned in our Chapter 4 discussion of events and delegates, event handlers in VB must be declared using the Handles keyword, and must accept two arguments: System.Object and System.EventArgs.
3. The event subroutine is called Button1_Click and not Command1_Click, because the Windows Form Designer gives buttons the default name ButtonXXX, as opposed to CommandXXX in VB6.
4. All of the code is contained in a class called Form1, which inherits from the Windows.Forms.Form class. (VB developers

unfamiliar with the concept of inheritance can consult an online explanation at ⊶CNNET070001.)

5. There is a curious boxed and grayed-out section called "Windows Form Designer generated code."

When the WFD created the empty form for us (it did this by default when we created the project), it generated the Form1 class code behind the scenes. When we added a button to the form, the WFD inserted a private member variable class called Button1 into the Form1 class. This may not seem obvious looking at the code in Figure 7.5, but you can see it if you expand the "Windows Form Designer generated code" section, as depicted in Figure 7.6.

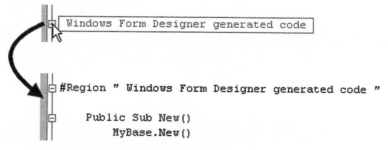

Figure 7.6   Expanding the WFD generated code

If you expand the WFD section, you will see that the WFD code is enclosed within #Region and #End Region tags. Scanning through this code (there is a lot of it), you will see the following two lines:

```
Private WithEvents Button1
As System.Windows.Forms.Button
...
Me.Button1 = New System.Windows.Forms.Button()
```

The first line declares the button class, while the second instantiates it. Notice that the button is declared with the WithEvents keyword, allowing the button class to receive events from the form, such as mouse clicks (see Visual Basic Events in Chapter 4 for an explanation of the WithEvents keyword). Look closely and you will see that the second line is contained in a private subroutine called InitializeComponent(). This subroutine is called from the form's New() method, which is similar to the Form_Initialize method in VB6 (it is called before the form loads). The New() method is also contained in the Windows Form Designer section that you expanded above:

```
Public Sub New()
  MyBase.New()
  'This call is required by the Windows Form Designer.
  InitializeComponent()

  'Add any initialization after the call to
  'InitializeComponent()
End sub
```

The InitializeComponent() method instantiates and configures all of the form's contained classes (buttons, labels, pictures, etc.). If you look in this method, for example, you will see the following lines that determine the button's size and location.

```
Me.Button1.Location = New System.Drawing.Point(80, 20)
Me.Button1.Size = New System.Drawing.Size(120, 50)
```

These lines were generated by the WFD when you placed the button on the form. If you were to return to the form and resize the button, the WFD would change the second line of code to match your actions. Visual Basic developers should notice that a control's location and size are now specified using the Location and Size properties (although the Windows Forms classes still expose the Left, Top, Height, and Width properties for backwards compatibility).

You may be wondering whether we can do the reverse—that is, can we change the underlying code and see a corresponding change in the button's size in the design environment? We can, but it is not advisable. The WFD doesn't expect you to modify the code it generates; if you make a change it doesn't understand, it could damage your entire project file. For demonstration purposes, however, let's do something innocuous and change the first parameter in the button's size from 120 to 200. Return to the design environment and the button's width will have increased.

Look (but don't touch!) through the rest of the WFD generated code and you will begin to understand the intricacies of the Windows Forms classes. Notice that the Form1 class has no Close() method, which may seem odd given that we used this method to close the form and terminate our application. Remember from Figure 7.2 that Form1 inherits from the Form class, which itself inherits from the ContainerControl class and so on. Our Form1 class thus inherited the Close() method of the Form class as well as additional methods and events that VB developers expect (Activate, Hide, KeyDown, KeyPress, etc.).

The code generated by the WFD in our example was VB code. Remember that the WFD is capable of producing C# code as well. You can see this by starting a C# Windows application project and repeating the actions of this example (placing a button on the form and so forth). Double-click the button and insert the following line in the button's event procedure:

```
private void button1_Click(object sender,
System.EventArgs e) {
  'this in C# is equivalent to "me" in VB
  this.Close();
}
```

The application is now equivalent to the VB example in Figure 7.4, the only difference being that the WFD generated C# code for us instead of VB. In both VB and C#, the WFD encloses the code it generates with the #Region and #End Region tags. If you examine the WFD generated code, you will see C# equivalents of the VB code we examined earlier. For example, the button's size and location are now determined by the following lines:

```
this.button1.Location = new System.Drawing.Point(
  80, 20);
this.button1.Size = new System.Drawing.Size(120, 50);
```

There are a few differences, however. The following line may catch your attention:

```
this.button1.Click += new
System.EventHandler(this.button1_Click);
```

Remember from our discussion of events and delegates in Chapter 4 that an event is a special type of delegate. While VB abstracts this relationship with its WithEvents and Handles keywords (look at Figure 7.5) , C# must use the underlying delegate up front. The line above registers the button1_Click() method with Button1's click delegate so that it is called when Button1 is clicked (say that five times fast).

Also note that the Form does not have a New() method like the VB example. In C#, the form's constructor serves the same purpose, calling InitializeComponent() and housing any initialization code you give the form. The C# code generated by the WFD is more revealing than the VB code it produces. The following C# code, for example, is not found in the previous VB example we created:

```
static void Main() {
  Application.Run(new Form1());
}
```

This code starts the application by calling the static `Run()` method of the `Application` class found in the `System.Windows.Forms` namespace, accepting as a parameter the startup form of the application. VB developers should realize that VB.NET implicitly adds the following code (though you will not see it) to the startup form of their projects:

```
Shared Sub Main()
  Application.Run(New Form1())
End Sub
```

It is possible for VB developers to override this method to determine how an application starts. You could, for example, put initialization code into this `Main()` method before the form loads and runs. For VB examples that override this method, see ∞⤳NET070002.

VB developers should keep in mind that they do not have to examine the code generated by the WFD; they can develop as they always did, knowing that the WFD is taking care of the details behind the scenes. The biggest change for VB developers will be getting used to the differences between the Windows Forms classes and the intrinsic controls in previous versions of VB. In the online article at ∞⤳NET070003, we discuss many of these intrinsic VB controls changes, as well as numerous new controls exposed by the Windows Forms classes.

Topic: Visual Inheritance

Thus far, most of this chapter has focused on using Windows Forms to create traditional GUIs: we have not done anything we couldn't have accomplished using unmanaged alternatives such as VB6 or MFC. The real benefit of the Windows Forms classes becomes apparent when you recognize that they retain the virtues of managed execution, most notably crosslanguage inheritance. As the upcoming example will illustrate, it is possible to create a GUI in one language and extend it in another. And when inheriting a GUI, you not only inherit its physical structure (control locations and sizes) but its associated code as well.

You have, in a sense, already used visual inheritance. Consider the application we created at the beginning of this chapter (depicted in Figure 7.4). When we created this project the VS.NET IDE automatically created a form for us (called Form1) that inherited from the System Form class:

```
Public Class Form1
  Inherits System.Windows.Forms.Form
```

In this case, the inheritance was implicit; VS.NET did it for us behind the scenes. The System Form class is just an abstract definition of a form without any contained controls such as buttons or textboxes. If we wanted, we could instruct Form1 to inherit from some other form we created (say Form2). By doing this, Form1 would not only inherit the attributes of Form2 (its size, location, etc.) but would also inherit any controls it contained.

The most important facet of visual inheritance is the accessibility of inherited controls. If Form1 inherited a button, for example, could we change its size and modify its event code? As we will see, this depends on the accessibility of the control in the inherited form (Form2). If Button1 is private, then it is off limits—we can look but not touch. If it is public, then we can modify it however we desire. This is illustrated in the following example.

EXAMPLE

In this example we will create a simple GUI in VB.NET, and then extend it in C#. Complete source code for both projects can be found at ^{CN}NET070010.

To begin, create a Visual Basic project in VS.NET. Instead of selecting the Windows Application template, however, select ClassLibrary (see Figure 7.3). A ClassLibrary is an assembly that is compiled as a DLL file and exposes classes that can be used in other programs.

After selecting the ClassLibrary template, go to the Project menu, select Add Windows Form, and call your form MyBaseForm. Resize the form and give it a button so that it resembles the form in Figure 7.4. Double-click the button and insert the following line of code, which will be executed when the button is clicked.

```
Private Sub Button1_Click(ByVal sender As System.Object,
ByVal e As System.EventArgs) Handles Button1.Click
  MsgBox("myBaseClass code: Button1 was clicked")
End Sub
```

Listing 7.2   Event code for Button1

Compile the ClassLibrary by going to the Build menu and selecting Build Solution. You now have an assembly DLL file that exposes the `MyBaseForm` class. You can verify this by using the ILDASM utility to inspect the assembly, which is located in the `\YourProjectDirectory\bin` directory.

Like all managed classes, `MyBaseForm` now exists as IL code and can be inherited by any managed language. Save your project and create a new C# Windows Application project. VS.NET will automatically create an empty form for us called Form1. We will not be using this form (we will create an inherited form momentarily), so right-click `Form1.cs` in the Solution Explorer window and select "Exclude from Project." Now go to the Project menu and select Add Inherited Form. Call your form `MyInheritedForm` and click Open. VS.NET will now invoke a tool called the Inheritance Picker, which will allow you to choose the form you wish to inherit from.

Click Browse and select the assembly DLL we previously created (remember, it is contained in the `\YourProjectDirectory\bin` directory). The Inheritance Picker will examine the assembly and ask you to choose which form you wish to inherit from (see Figure 7.7).

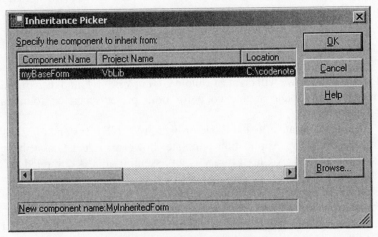

Figure 7.7   VS.NET's Inheritance Picker

Select `myBaseForm` and click OK. VS.NET will now create a form called `MyInheritedForm` that inherits from `myBaseForm`, something you can verify by examining the underlying code in your project:

```
public class MyInheritedForm : VbLib.myBaseForm
```

Experiment with `MyInheritedForm` for a moment and you will find that you cannot resize Button1 or modify any of its properties (they will all be grayed out in the properties toolbox). If you attempt to click the button, VS.NET will politely inform you that it is inaccessible by graying out its border (see Figure 7.8).

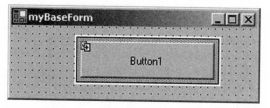

Figure 7.8   An inaccessible inherited control

If you consult the original VB.NET ClassLibrary, however, you will see that this behavior is expected. Examine the code for `MyBaseForm` (open the WFD generated code) and you will see the following line:

```
Private WithEvents Button1 As System.Windows.Forms.Button
```

As can be seen, Button1 is a private member variable of `MyBaseForm`. It should come as no surprise, therefore, that it is off limits; object-oriented principles tell us that although class inheritance inherits private member variables and methods, they are not accessible in the child class (`MyInheritedForm` in our case). As such, Button1 is completely inaccessible in the design environment—we can't even attach event code to it. The only time the button is accessible is when the application runs. Run the application by pressing F5, click Button1, and you will see the message shown in Figure 7.9.

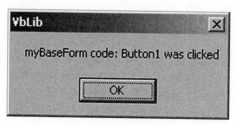

Figure 7.9   Inheriting MyBaseForm's code

If we wish to allow Button1 to be modified, we must make it accessible in the child class by making it public. We could do this by loading our VB.NET ClassLibrary and changing the `Private` keyword in Button1's declaration to `Public`. Remember, however, that this line was generated by the WFD, and changing its code is not a good idea. A safer approach is to change the button's `Modifiers` property to `Public` using the property toolbox in the design environment. After doing this, rebuild the ClassLibrary and then reload the C# project application.

You will notice that the button can now be resized, its properties are accessible, and we can even attach event code to it. When VS.NET loaded our C# application, it consulted the VB.NET ClassLibrary and determined that Button1 was now public. Double-click Button1 and give it the following event code:

```
private void Button1_Click_1(object sender,
System.EventArgs e)
{
   MessageBox.Show("myInheritedClass code: " +
      "Button1 was clicked");
}
```

Note that in C# we cannot use the `MsgBox` command available in VB.NET (which is provided for compatibility with VB6); we must use the MessageBox class in the Runtime classes. Also note that the method is called `Button1_Click_1`, as opposed to `Button1_Click` in Listing 7.2. Both these methods are now associated with the button's click event. If you run the application and click Button1 you will see two messages: the one in Figure 7.10 and one that contains the message above.

You may be wondering if you can suppress the base class's event code. That is, can we prevent the message in Figure 7.9 from being displayed? This is possible, provided that the base class's event handler for Button1 is `Public`. Look in Listing 7.2, however, and you will see that it is `Private`, so we are out of luck—the message will always be displayed when the button is clicked. If the method were `Public` (if the base class author explicitly made it `Public` in Listing 7.2), we could suppress the message by "unregistering" the base class's delegate with the button's click event:

```
this.Button1.Click -= new
System.EventHandler(this.Button1_Click);
```

Adding this line of code to Form1's `InitializeComponent()` method suppresses the base class's event code. You may find it confusing that the method in Listing 7.2 is private, even though we switched the button's `Modifiers` property to Public. All the `Modifiers` property determines, however, is whether or not objects can be modified in the inherited class;

it doesn't say anything about the base class's event handlers. By default, all the event handlers of a form are private. To make them suppressible by inheriting forms, you must explicitly make them Public.

It is important to realize that base class's author prescribes what can and cannot be done with the GUI. If you don't want a form's control to be modified, for example, set its modifiers property to Private. Likewise, for controls where modification is permissible, set their modifiers properties to Public. The modifiers property can also be set to Assembly or Family. Assembly makes the control accessible only to those entities within the same assembly, while Family makes it accessible only to the class and its decedents.

Visual inheritance can be useful when you have a collection of forms that share common physical and behavioral characteristics. You could create a base form to embody these overlapping attributes and then have multiple child forms inherit from it. If one of these characteristics then changes—if a common button must be renamed or its event code rewritten—you only have to change the base form; the descendent classes will automatically inherit the modification. Also keep in mind that visual inheritance doesn't have to stop here; the descendent classes can in turn be inherited by other forms, and so on. Any change in the base class would be reflected right down the class hierarchy.

HOW AND WHY

How Do I Call a Base Class's Method When I Override It?

If you override a method of an inherited class, it is often desirable to ensure that the method you are overriding is called by its replacement. Assume, for example, that we added the following code to the myBaseForm class in Figure 7.4:

```
Protected Overrides Sub OnClosed(ByVal e As
System.EventArgs)
  MsgBox("myBaseForm: Form is about to close.")
End Sub
```

The OnClosed() method is automatically invoked when the form is closed. Although the code above displays a message box, it would more likely house cleanup routines for the form itself (release resources, etc.). If we were to inherit the Visual Basic form into the C# program depicted in Figure 7.8, the OnClosed() method above would get called when the application shuts down.

We could override this method in the inheriting form by using the override keyword. We should ensure that the `OnClosed()` method we are replacing is also called, using the `base` keyword:

```
protected override void OnClosed(System.EventArgs e)
{
  MessageBox.Show("myInheritedForm: " +
    "Form is about to close");
  // must call the base's OnClosed method too!
  base.OnClosed(e);
}
```

Two message boxes will thus be displayed when the form closes. In this example, it is not necessary to call the base class's method (doing so would merely suppress the first message box). If the first `OnClosed()` method contained vital cleanup code for the application, however, it would be necessary to call it from the derived class as we have illustrated, a practice you should follow when dealing with the Windows Forms classes.

SUMMARY

Because the Windows Forms classes exist as managed IL code, they can be inherited across languages. Visual inheritance can either be done programmatically or using VS.NET's Inheritance Picker. When you inherit a form, you inherit its physical attributes, the controls it contains, and the code associated with the controls and the form itself. Like any class in the managed environment, the ability to modify the members of an inherited class depends on their accessibility. If a form's button is private, for example, it cannot be modified when the form is inherited; if it is public, then it can. Using these rules, a designer can choose those portions of a GUI that can be changed when inherited.

Chapter Summary

Windows Forms are a set of classes in the `System.Windows.Forms` namespace that are used to create desktop GUIs for the managed environment. An integral part of Windows Forms is the Windows Form Designer (WFD) tool of VS.NET, which allows you to graphically construct GUIs as you can in VB6. When you resize a form or give it a label, the WFD generates code that utilizes the Windows Forms classes (in either VB.NET or C#) to reflect your actions. VB developers must familiarize themselves with the way these classes have changed from intrinsic VB6 controls; the frame control, for example, must be replaced with either the GroupBox or Panel classes.

Windows Forms classes can be inherited across languages because they exist as language neutral IL code. A GUI developed in C# can be extended in Visual Basic, which can in turn be extended and used in managed C++. Inheriting a GUI not only inherits its physical characteristics but the GUI's code as well. Visual inheritance adheres to the rules of object inheritance: if a base form's control is marked Private, then it cannot be modified in the inherited form, but if it is marked Public, it can.

Chapter 8

—

ASP.NET

WHAT IS ASP/ASP.NET?

Given the complexity and sophistication of today's Web technologies, it can be hard to remember that in its infancy the Internet was arguably a glorified file-transfer system. Clients would request (and hopefully receive) files from servers using established transfer protocols such as FTP and gopher. Eventually, these binary protocols gave way to the Hyper Text Markup Language (HTML) protocol, which allowed formatted text to be transferred across the Internet. Clients would still request files from servers, but the files would be dynamically rendered on a browser, which would format the HTML into readable content.

The next step along the evolutionary ladder was the generation of dynamic content. Instead of providing clients with static files, servers would dynamically generate HTML files in response to a client's requests. Two of the earliest frameworks were the Common Gateway Interface (CGI) and Microsoft Active Server Pages (ASP). These frameworks allowed for dynamic content creation in response to user actions.

ASP.NET is Microsoft's new version of ASP for the managed environment. ASP.NET brings about significant changes from its predecessor, most notably by supporting strongly typed and precompiled languages such as C# and VB. With ASP.NET you can also design web application GUIs using the drag-and-drop form design approach that made Visual Basic popular.

ASP.NET is a server-side technology that requires the installation of

Microsoft Internet Information Server (IIS). Without IIS installed, you will not be able to build or test the examples in this chapter.

PROBLEMS WITH TRADITIONAL ASP

In the Introduction to Chapter 6, we compared ADO with ADO.NET. In this section, we similarly examine the limitations of ASP in order to appreciate its evolved .NET manifestation.

1. ASP only supports scripting languages.

    ASP scripting code is usually written in languages such as JScript or VBScript. Typically, these languages provide only a subset of the functionality exposed by a complete development language (such as Java or Visual Basic). Scripting languages such as JScript and VBScript are also weakly-typed. This means that all variables are Variants (generic types). Also, no type-checking is done at design time, which often results in error-prone code.

    The performance of ASP script code also suffers because it is interpreted. Unlike desktop applications that are fully compiled, ASP scripts are translated one line at a time by the ASP runtime, degrading performance. Interpreted scripting code also raises debugging issues. If line 50 of an ASP script contains a syntax error, it will not be caught until the previous 49 lines have executed. Modern development environments, in contrast, will catch all of a program's syntax errors in a single compilation step.

2. Script Code is combined with the HTML interface.

    ASP files frequently combine script code with HTML. This results in ASP scripts that are lengthy, difficult to read, and switch frequently between code and HTML. The interspersion of HTML with ASP code is particularly problematic for larger web applications, where content must be kept separate from business logic.

3. COM Administration

    Because ASP only supports scripting languages, developers frequently move logic into COM components and then call them from ASP scripts. By writing COM components in languages such as C++, developers can leverage the strongly-typed features that are absent from ASP.

    Problems with the COM/ASP hybrid arise, however, when a COM component evolves and must be updated. Because the

ASP runtime may keep objects loaded in memory, updating a COM component can require shutting down the web server (IIS) and possibly re-registering the component with the Windows Registry. This scenario is unacceptable for large, high-traffic web applications where reliable service is paramount.

4. Application configuration is stored in a proprietary format that is not easily ported to different machines.

The configuration information for an ASP web application (such as session state and server timeouts) is stored in the IIS metabase. Because the metabase is stored in a proprietary format, it can only be modified on the server machine with utilities such as the Internet Service Manager. With limited support for programmatically manipulating or extracting these settings, it is often an arduous task to port an ASP application from one server to another.

INTRODUCING ASP.NET

With .NET, Microsoft has completely redesigned ASP to address its limitations. To accomplish this task, backwards-compatibility with ASP had to be sacrificed. As we will see, migrating ASP scripts to the managed environment is not always a straightforward task.

Since ASP is in such wide use, however, Microsoft ensured that ASP scripts execute without modification on a machine with the .NET Framework (the ASP engine, ASP.DLL, is not modified when installing the .NET Framework). Thus, IIS can house both ASP and ASP.NET scripts on the same machine.

Among the advantages ASP.NET boasts over ASP are the following:

1. Separation of code from content. ASP.NET allows the developer to separate script code from HTML. This allows for a clean separation of code from content and formatting and promotes code reuse.

2. Support for compiled languages. While ASP.NET still supports the traditional set of scripting languages, support is also provided for fully compiled languages. Instead of using VBScript, a developer can use VB.NET and access features such as strong typing and object-oriented programming.

Using compiled languages also means that ASP.NET pages do not suffer the performance penalties associated with interpreted code. ASP.NET pages are precompiled to byte-code and Just In Time (JIT) compiled when first requested. Subsequent requests are directed to the fully compiled code, which is cached until the source changes.

3. Greater support for different browsers via server-side controls and events. Following object-oriented design principles, ASP.NET pages make use of server-side controls called ASP.NET web controls. These controls are instantiated on the server, and like regular objects they have associated methods, properties, and events. The advantage of server-side controls is that they render themselves on the client as standard HTML 3.2 (and optionally DHTML), depending on the capabilities of the client browser. In other words, an advanced browser will automatically receive advanced features, while an older browser will still receive readable HTML. Since the controls reside completely on the server and send standard HTML to the client, browsers can be completely unaware of the .NET Runtime. Thus, virtually any browser can access an ASP.NET page.

4. Intuitive GUI design. With ASP.NET you can design web applications as you did in Visual Basic 6, by dragging and dropping GUI elements in a sophisticated design environment. The next topic in this chapter demonstrates this feature.

As you will see throughout this chapter, almost every new feature introduced with ASP.NET is designed to provide tremendous improvements for rapid web application development. The advanced GUI design, separation of code from content, encapsulation of HTML, and masking of client-side/server-side issues makes ASP.NET a very powerful platform for designing web pages.

CORE CONCEPTS

Caching
ASP.NET's improved caching techniques will help you build more scalable and high-performance web applications. ASP.NET offers three types of caching:

1. Page-level: With page-level caching, dynamic page output is cached and served directly on subsequent requests. ASP.NET thus does not have to regenerate dynamic content on every request, which can significantly reduce load time. With this type of caching, you specify an expiration policy that determines how long a given page is maintained in the output cache. It is important to note that the output cache does *not* contain com-

piled page code (there is a separate cache used exclusively by the ASP.NET Runtime for this purpose). Rather, the output cache contains the HTML (and possibly DHTML) generated by the compiled ASP.NET page code.

2. Fragment: Fragment caching allows the developer to explicitly cache only portions of a page. Quite often, a certain portion of a page *must* be dynamically generated on every request (a real-time stock quote for example). By using fragment caching, a developer can separate those portions of the page that are static and can be cached from those that require dynamic generation. This sort of caching can provide tremendous improvements in page access speeds.

3. The Cache API: The ASP.NET Framework exposes a rich Cache API that gives developers the ability to manually cache frequently requested data. The Cache API gives developers direct access to ASP.NET's cache engine, which can be used to design custom caching solutions where page-level and fragment caching are inadequate.

For more details on ASP.NET's caching abilities, as well as examples, please consult ⟲NET080012.

SIMPLE APPLICATION

In this example we will create a simple ASP.NET page that can be used to register a user with a website. Before continuing, make sure you have IIS installed. IIS can be installed from the Windows Control Panel by choosing Add/Remove Programs → Add/Remove Windows Components, and selecting Internet Information Services (IIS). Figure 8.1 depicts the interface for our first ASP.NET page.

To build this example, open your favorite text editor, create a file named register.aspx, and save it to its own directory (say, C:\asp Intro). Note that ASP.NET scripts end with the extension .aspx, while ASP scripts end with .asp. Because these file extensions are kept distinct, IIS can invoke the older ASP engine when ASP scripts are referenced and the ASP.NET Runtime for .aspx files.

In the register.aspx file (also available online at ⟲NET080001), add the following code:

```
<HTML><HEAD><TITLE>ASP.NET Example</TITLE></HEAD>
<BODY>
```

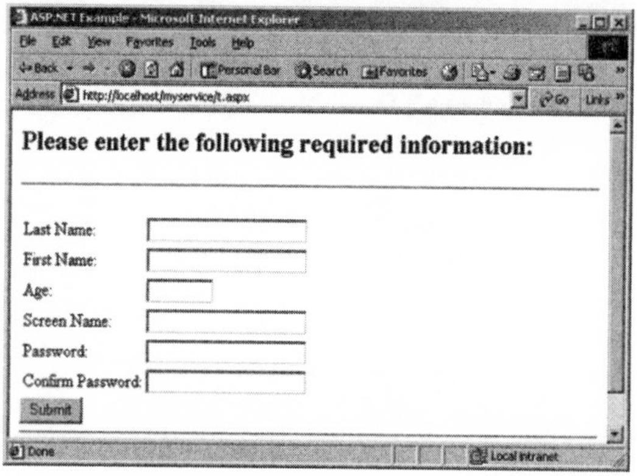

Figure 8.1   Our first ASP.NET application

```
<H2>Please enter the following required
information:</H2>
<hr>
<form runat="server">
<table>
<tr>
<td>Last Name:</td><td><asp:TextBox id="txtLName"
runat="server" size=20 /></td>
</tr>
<tr>
<td>First Name:</td><td><asp:TextBox id="txtFName"
runat="server" size=20 /></td>
</tr>
<tr>
<td>Age:</td><td><asp:TextBox id="txtAge" runat="server"
size=5 /></td>
</tr>
<tr>
<td>Screen Name:</td><td><asp:TextBox id="txtSName"
runat="server" size=20 /></td>
</tr>
<tr>
<td>Password:</td><td><asp:TextBox id="txtPassWd"
TextMode="Password" runat="server" size=20 /></td>
</tr>
<tr>
<td>Confirm Password:</td><td><asp:TextBox
id="txtConfirm" TextMode="Password" runat="server"
size=20 /></td>
```

```
</tr>
</table>
<asp:Button Text="Submit" OnClick="OnSubmit"
runat="server" />
<hr>
<asp:Label id="txtOutput" runat="server" />
</form>
</BODY>

<script language="C#" runat="server">
  void OnSubmit (Object sender, EventArgs e)
  {
    txtOutput.Text = "Successfully registered user: " +
      txtLName.Text + ", " + txtFName.Text;
  }
</script>
</HTML>
```

Listing 8.1   register.aspx

As you can see, this file contains a mix of HTML, specialized ASP tags (in an XML format), and C# code. The important sections are discussed below.

WEB CONTROLS

ASP developers will note several features that differentiate register .aspx from a typical ASP script. First, look closely at the runat=server attributes bolded in Listing 8.1, which tell ASP.NET to run these lines on the server. We applied this attribute on numerous controls that are prefixed with the asp: keyword. For example:

```
<asp:Label id="txtOutput" runat="server"/>
```

It may seem confusing that we are specifying that a control (a label, in this case) should run at the server. What we are seeing, however, is something called a "web control," which does exactly that. When ASP.NET processes register.aspx, it sees that txtOutput is a web control because of the asp: prefix. As a result, it generates client-side HTML code that renders a label on the browser.

Those familiar with HTML may be wondering why we didn't simply write an HTML label ourselves, instead of having ASP.NET generate one for us. The answer is that web controls are more sophisticated than their intrinsic HTML equivalents. We can do things very easily with a web control (resize it as we please, attach event code to it) that require considerably more effort to code in HTML. By using web controls we shift the burden of HTML specifics onto ASP.NET, which automatically converts our control into HTML that the browser can understand.

Also note that the Submit button registers the OnSubmit() handler for the OnClick event. The OnSubmit() method is defined inside the <script> tag as part of the server-side code. Event handlers for ASP.NET controls are defined in the same format as Windows Forms controls examined in Chapter 7. Refer to the Overview Example in Chapter 7 for the specifics of declaring event handlers for the .NET Framework.

As can be seen from Listing 8.1, OnSubmit() accepts two parameters: *sender* of type Object, and *e* as type EventArgs. Recall from Chapter 7 that sender is a reference to the object that raised the event. The EventArgs parameter contains additional event-specific information, such as which mouse button was clicked (on a mouse-click event). The EventArgs class is detailed at <website>. One can see that Windows Forms and Web Forms are very similar—truly highlighting how .NET closely unifies the web design model with traditional desktop application development.

The next topic on ASP.NET will highlight the advantages of web controls.

CREATING THE VIRTUAL DIRECTORY

To access the code we created in Listing 8.1, we must create a virtual root on the IIS web server where the page will reside. Open the Internet Services Manager by going to Start → Settings → Control Panel → Administrative Tools → Internet Services Manager. (Refer to Figure 8.2.)

Click on Default Web Site, and right-click in the directory view. Select New → Virtual Directory from the pop-up menu. This will launch the Virtual Directory Creation Wizard. You will be prompted to enter the physical directory where the web content is stored (enter C:\aspIntro). In addition, you will be asked to give an alias for the directory (enter aspIntro). This alias is simply a short-hand mapping to the physical directory. You will navigate to this alias in your web browser. Click Finish and test the ASP.NET page by launching Internet Explorer and navigating to: http://localhost/aspIntro/register.aspx.

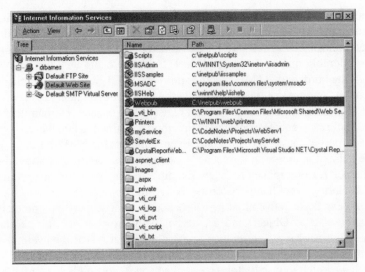

Figure 8.2   Creating a virtual directory

ANALYZING THE OUTPUT

After ASP.NET processes the .aspx file, you will see the interface depicted in Figure 8.1. If you look at the client-side code that was generated (by selecting View → Source from the Internet Explorer menu), you will notice that the source behind the interface is quite different from the code we wrote in Listing 8.1. First, all the `runat=server` tags are not present. This should come as no surprise, since these lines were executed at the server and we are inspecting client code.

If you examine the client code further, you will note that all of the web controls in Listing 8.1 (denoted by the `asp:` prefix) have been converted into HTML equivalents. For example, the `<asp:TextBox id="txtFName"...>` line has been changed to: `<input name="txtFName" type="text" id="txtFName" size="20" />`. This change highlights the fact that web controls are processed at the server and automatically rendered as regular HTML on the client.

WEB CONTROLS AND HIDDEN FIELDS

Enter values in the `Name` and `Age` text fields, click on the `Submit` button, and you will notice some interesting behavior. The ASP.NET page contacts the server, and as expected the message "Successfully registered user . . ." appears at the bottom of the page. If you look carefully, however, you will notice that the values you entered in the text fields at the top of the form do not disappear (they persist across the request to the server). Had we developed this application in ASP, these text boxes would have been empty; the page refresh would have cleared the values. Normal HTML controls are inherently stateless; maintaining state (i.e., the values of a controls or variables) would require extra client-side script.

We did not, however, include any state code in Listing 8.1. One of the virtues of a web control is that it automatically maintains state between server invocations. But how does a web control do this, given that it is ultimately converted into client-side HTML, which itself is stateless? If you look once again at the client source, you will notice a line similar to the following:

```
<input type="hidden" name="__VIEWSTATE" value="dDw4ODkyMzg3MDA70z4=" />
```

ASP.NET generated this line, which creates a hidden HTML control called __VIEWSTATE in the client. The purpose of the control is to maintain the state of web controls across server invocations. Don't worry about the details of how Framework uses __VIEWSTATE (it is proprietary and subject to change). Just realize that ASP.NET is performing some HTML tricks behind the scenes to give your web controls characteristics that would be otherwise difficult to obtain.

SCRIPTS AND LANGUAGES

Look back at Listing 8.1 and you will see the <script> tag in the .aspx file. This tag must be specified before we write our ASP.NET code. Scripts in ASP.NET are declared using the following notation:

```
<script language="C#" runat="server">
```

Underneath the <script> tag in Listing 8.1 is our actual ASP.NET script. Note that this script uses the C# syntax. As mentioned earlier, ASP.NET supports strongly-typed, fully compiled languages. The language attribute of the <script> tag tells ASP.NET which compiler to use when building the ASP.NET page. For example, language="VB" is used when the server-side code is written in VB.NET.

The runat=server attribute specifies that the compiled code should reside on the server. If you take a look at the client-side source again (select View → Source in Internet Explorer) you will notice that the `<script>` tag does not appear in the client. The client simply forwards all requests to the server, where the code to process the request resides.

The script code in Listing 8.1 follows the same strongly-typed syntax we have used to create standard .NET components through this Code-Note. This may not come as a surprise for developers new to web development, but it is a feature ASP developers have long desired. Consider the following fragment, which is how the script of Listing 8.1 would be written in standard ASP:

```
<%
  Response.Write( "Successfully registered user: " & _
    Request.Form("txtLName") & ", " &
    Request.Form("txtFName"))
  ...
%>
```

One major problem with the weakly-typed scripting language of ASP is that references are not checked at compile-time. In the code above, if we had incorrectly referenced the `txtLName` control as `txtLName2`, our error wouldn't have been caught until a user requested the page. As we will see in the next topic, syntactical errors can be caught at compile-time with ASP.NET.

SUMMARY

This example barely scratches the surface of ASP.NET's capabilities. In the following topic, we will see how we can use the VS.NET IDE to intuitively design a web page in a fashion similar to building a Visual Basic 6 application.

Topic: VS.NET Web Forms

One of the most compelling features of ASP.NET is that you can design web application GUIs as you do in Visual Basic 6, by placing and resizing controls graphically. And, unlike with traditional web design tools such as FrontPage and ColdFusion, you can also attach event code to the GUI elements in your application.

We first looked at the VS.NET IDE in Chapter 7 (Windows Forms). If you haven't already done so, now would be a good time to read Chapter 7 to familiarize yourself with the VS.NET IDE. We saw that whenever you design a desktop GUI in the VS.NET IDE, the Windows Form Designer (WFD) translates your actions into code that utilizes the System .Windows.Forms classes. The premise behind Web Forms is similar; you design a web GUI in the same intuitive manner you used in Chapter 7. The difference with Web Forms is that the code uses System.Web.UI classes to automatically generate user-interface code.

WEB FORMS EXAMPLE

Building the Application

To write a web application with Web Forms, start the VS.NET and then go to the File menu and select New and then Project. This will bring up the New Project screen that we saw way back in Figure 7.3. Select web application under Template and give your project the name MyWebApp (the project location will default to http://localhost; ignore this for the time being).

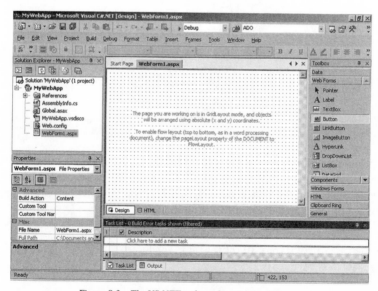

Figure 8.3   The VS.NET web application environment

After a few moments, the VS.NET IDE will present you with a screen that resembles the one in Figure 8.3.

Take a minute to investigate the new VS.NET web application environment. As you can see, it strongly resembles the Windows Form environment that we saw in Chapter 7. A toolbox to right of the screen exposes controls such as buttons and textboxes. To the bottom left of the screen a Property Inspector, similar to the one found in Visual Basic, shows the properties of the currently selected object. In the center of the screen, however, a blank page exists in place of the expected windows form. Think of this page as the web equivalent of a desktop form; you place controls on this page, which represents the viewable area of the web application.

Click the page in the middle of the screen, then look at the language property in the property inspector. You can set this property to C#, JavaScript, or VB, to determine the type of code the Web Form Designer will generate. Keep this property set to C#.

Adding Controls

To create your first web application in the VS.NET IDE, drag both a Textbox and Button control onto the page, so you have something that resembles Figure 8.4.

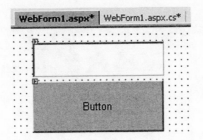

Figure 8.4   VS.NET web application

The button will have the default name Button1, and the textbox will have the default name TextBox1. For now, leave these names intact. Double-click on the button to bring up the code window and insert the following code into the button's event handler:

```
private void Button1_Click(object sender,
System.EventArgs e)
{
   TextBox1.Text = "My Second Web Application!";
}
```

Listing 8.2   Button event handler

You have now written your first web application from within the VS.NET IDE. Look at the other code surrounding your event handler, however, and (if you've read Chapter 7) you might have a feeling of déjà vu. First, notice the #region and #end region tags that denote code automatically generated by the Web Form Designer. Scroll to near the top of the code and you will see the following:

```
public class WebForm1 : System.Web.UI.Page
{
  protected System.Web.UI.WebControls.TextBox TextBox1;
  protected System.Web.UI.WebControls.Button Button1;
  ...
}
```

Listing 8.3   The Page class

Just as the System.Windows.Form class represents a form for desktop applications, the System.Web.UI.Page class is the basis for web pages designed in the VS.NET IDE. When we created the project, the Web Form Designer automatically generated the WebForm1 class that inherited from the Page class. Likewise, when you added the textbox and button to your page, the Web Form Designer gave the WebForm1 class the TextBox1 and Button1 classes as shown above.

Remember, ASP.NET is built upon web controls, which dynamically generate client-side HTML. By constructing your application graphically as you just did, you are implicitly describing the HTML that clients will see. The good news is that you do not have to concern yourself with the underlying HTML. Simply design your application in the VS.NET IDE, and the Web Form Designer will do the hard work of creating client-side HTML that reflects your design.

Running the Example

To run your web application, press F5 from within the VS.NET IDE. After a moment, VS.NET will invoke a web browser that automatically navigates to the following URL: http://localhost/MyWebApp/WebForm1.aspx. The application you designed in Figure 8.4 will appear inside the browser. If you click the button, "My Second Web Application!" will appear in the textbox. It is tempting to think that this code is executing entirely on the client, but in reality:

1. Clicking the button sends an HTTP Post request back to the web server (IIS);
2. The web server determines that the post is intended for an aspx file, so it invokes the ASP.NET Runtime;
3. The ASP.NET Runtime determines that Button1 was clicked, so it invokes the Button1_Click method in your application;

4. The `Button1_Click` method changes the `Text` property of TextBox1 to "My Second Web Application!" and

5. The ASP.NET generates client-side HTML for both the `Button` and `TextBox` web controls. Because the TextBox's caption was changed in Step 4, new equivalent HTML is generated and appears in the browser.

To emphasize the server-side interplay that is occurring, add the following line of code to the `Button1_Click()` event in Listing 8.2:

```
TextBox1.Width = (int)TextBox1.Width.Value + 50;
```

Rerun the application and you will observe some amusing behavior: the textbox will successively increase its width as you click the button. Remember, the code is executing on the server. In Step 4 above, the Button's code now also changes the TextBox's width. This, in turn, influences the client-side HTML, resulting in the dynamically changing textbox in your browser.

You are encouraged to explore the other web controls in the VS.NET IDE, such as the Table, RadioButton, and CheckBox controls. These controls, coupled with the event code that you can attach to them, makes developing web applications as straightforward as desktop design in VB6.

DEBUGGING AND BREAKPOINTS

One of the advantages of ASP.NET over ASP is the ability to compile an application prior to deploying it. This capability ensures that a script is free of syntax errors before it is deployed (logical errors, of course, must be detected through testing). If, for example, we incorrectly referenced `TextBox1` in Listing 8.2 as `TextBox2`, when we attempt to run the application (by hitting F5), ASP.NET will inform us:

```
The type or namespace name 'TextBox2' could not be found ...
```

ASP.NET gives one all the capabilities of a modern development environment. You can add a breakpoint to the same line in Listing 8.2 by right-clicking the line and selecting Insert Breakpoint. Run the application by clicking F5, then click the button in the browser. Instead of updating the textbox as one might expect, you will return to the VS.NET environment. Here, you can inspect program variables, step through the rest of the program, make changes, and continue.

PAGE DIRECTIVES

If you compare our development efforts in this section with those of the Simple Application in Listing 8.1, you will note that:

1. We did not have to write a messy .asmx file.
2. We did not have to create a virtual directory.

Both of these points are virtues of the VS.NET IDE. The IDE will automatically create .asmx files and a virtual directory to house the files for us. Recall from the previous example that a virtual directory really maps to a physical directory somewhere on the computer. At the beginning of this example, when we created the project, VS.NET put it in http://localhost. This virtual directory usually maps to the C:\InetPub\wwwroot\ directory on the machine, meaning that our project's files can be found in: C:\InetPub\wwwroot\MyWebApp\. If you look in this directory, you will find files called WebForm1.asmx and WebForm1.asmx.cs, which were produced by the VS.NET as we developed our project. These files can be quite revealing if you examine them outside the design environment (using NOTEPAD, for example). Inspect Web-Form1.asmx, and at the top of the file you will see a line similar to the following:

```
<%@ Page language="c#" Codebehind="WebForm1.aspx.cs"
Inherits="MyWebApp.WebForm1" %>
```

This line is called a Page Directive, and it tells ASP.NET how the script should be compiled. The most important attribute in this directive is CodeBehind, which tells ASP.NET that a Page class is associated with this particular .aspx file. If you examine the WebForm1.aspx.cs file that Codebehind points to, you will see the source for the WebForm1 class in Listing 8.2. Thus, when you reference http://localhost/MyWebApp/WebForm1.aspx from within your browser, ASP.NET realizes that it has an associated class located in WebForm1.aspx.cs, JIT compiles it, and delivers the HTTP the class produces back to your browser.

HOW AND WHY

Can I Write My Own Web Controls?

You can write your own web controls by writing a class that inherits from the System.Web.UI.Control class. An example of a custom web control can be found at ○ᶜᴺ⤸NET080002.

What Kinds of Web Controls Are Shipped with ASP.NET?
ASP.NET ships with a variety of web controls to enhance the interactive nature of web applications. In the Simple Application of this chapter, you were introduced to ASP.NET intrinsic controls—controls that effectively wrap HTML equivalents. ASP.NET ships with packages of other controls, including rich controls, data controls, and validation controls. While a full description of each control shipped with ASP.NET is beyond the space considerations of this CodeNote, detailed documentation and examples can be obtained on the companion website, www.codenotes.com at ⌐CN⌐NET080003. Some of the web controls that ship with ASP.NET are described below:

- Rich controls: At the time of this writing, ASP.NET comes with two rich controls, namely the AdRotator and Calendar controls. The ad rotator provides a simple and flexible way to present advertisements on your site, while the Calendar acts as a highly customizable calendar control. Microsoft plans to ship ASP.NET with a variety of other rich controls. Rich controls essentially wrap complex HTML interfaces and control logic into reusable components. Examples of using the AdRotator and Calendar control can be found at ⌐CN⌐NET080003.

- Data controls: The heart of any enterprise system is its data. ASP.NET provides extensive facilities for binding relational and hierarchical (XML) data to web controls such as combo-boxes, check boxes, lists, and labels. ASP.NET also ships with several controls specifically designed for the display of data—the Repeater, DataList, and DataGrid. Each of these data controls is geared at a specific kind of data organization, but they give you the flexibility to customize their look-and-feel. Information and examples on ASP.NET data controls can be obtained at the following link: ⌐CN⌐NET080004.

- Validation controls: ASP.NET provides a collection of controls dedicated to validating user input. These controls are designed to maintain user-friendly website interaction as well as data integrity (when user input is fed into a database). You can use validation controls to quickly determine if a field is entered, and compare it against some value, range of values, or regular expression. The power of validation controls lies in their ability to be used in combination to quickly implement complex input validation. A complete discussion of validation controls is available at: ⌐CN⌐NET080005.

SUMMARY

Web controls are a quantum leap forward in rapid application design for the Web. With ASP.NET, you can build incredibly complex server-side forms using a paradigm familiar to anyone who has programmed in Visual Basic. Simply drag and drop controls on the form, add code to the various control events, and program in the language of your choice.

When a client requests the page, the ASP.NET Framework will automatically convert your controls and code into browser-appropriate HTML. In other words, application developers can once again concentrate on developing applications, without worrying about scripting, tags, or HTML.

Topic: ASP.NET Applications and Configuration

OVERVIEW

Like ASP, ASP.NET encapsulates its entities within a web application. A web application is an abstract term for all the resources available within the confines of an IIS virtual directory. For example, a web application may consist of one or more ASP.NET pages, assemblies, web services (see Chapter 9), configuration files, graphics, and more.

In this section we explore two fundamental components of a web application, namely global application files (Global.asax) and configuration files (Web.config).

Global.asax

Global.asax is a file used to declare application-level events and objects. Global.asax is the ASP.NET extension of the ASP Global.asa file. Code to handle application events (such as the start and end of an application) reside in Global.asax. Such event code cannot reside in the ASP.NET page or web service code itself, since during the start or end of the application, its code has not yet been loaded (or unloaded). Global.asax is also used to declare data that is available across different application requests or across different browser sessions. This process is known as application and session state management.

The Global.asax file must reside in the IIS virtual root. Remember that a virtual root can be thought of as the container of a web application. Events and state specified in the global file are then applied to all resources housed within the web application. If, for example, Global.asax defines a state application variable, all .aspx files within the virtual root will be able to access the variable.

Like an ASP.NET page, the Global.asax file is compiled upon the arrival of the first request for any resource in the application. The similarity continues when changes are made to the Global.asax file; ASP.NET automatically notices the changes, recompiles the file, and directs all new requests to the newest compilation. A Global.asax file is automatically created when you create a new web application project in the VS.NET IDE.

Global.asax files consist of the following elements:

1. Event Declarations: Define event delegates, such as OnStart(), that are global to an application (delegates are covered in Chapter 4).
2. Application Directives: Compiler-specific settings such as import statements.
3. Object Tag Declarations: Instances of objects that are globally accessible (state application variables).

All three elements are described in detail below.

Event Declarations

The ASP.NET Framework defines several event delegates specific to the application or session as a whole. These are events that are fired before or after an application resource, such as an ASP.NET page or web service, processes a request. For instance, code that is handled once for each user session is best handled in the Session_Start() method. The Session_Start() method is called, for example, when the user opens a new web browser session and navigates to a specific application resource.

The syntax follows the ASP.NET page syntax, as shown below:

```
<script language="C#" runat="server">
void Session_Start()
{
  // Code here that initializes a user settings or data
  // Executed once for each user (i.e. a browser client)
}
</script>
```

Listing 8.4   Session Start Event

Delegates exist for many other events, such as the `Application_Start()` method, which is executed when the application is first started by any client, or `Application_End()`, which is called when the application is shut down.

A list of all available delegates, typical functions, and applied examples can be obtained at ⊶NET080010.

Application Directives

Application directives are placed at the top of the Global.asax file and provide information used to compile the global file. Three application directives are defined, namely Application, Assembly, and Import. Each directive is applied with the following syntax:

```
<%@ appDirective appAttribute=Value ...%>
```

The Application directive has two corresponding attributes, which may be used individually or in combination:

1. Inherits: This attribute allows you to identify the base class that Global.asax will inherit from. For example, we might create a generic `CodeNotes.GlobalClass` that acts as a base class for all CodeNotes-specific web applications. By inheriting from this class, Global.asax can access all the methods and configuration information it exposes. The Global.asax files for each Code-Notes web application would begin with the following line:

```
<%@ Application Inherits="CodeNotes.GlobalClass" %>
```

2. Description: This attribute allows the programmer to add human-readable documentation to the Global.asax file. The Description attribute is ignored at compile time.

```
<%@ Application Description="Test harness for CodeNotes" %>
```

The Assembly directive is required to reference any assemblies used throughout the Global.asax file. This directive is analogous to the /reference switch available when compiling .NET components via the command line. If methods in Global.asax access SQL Server, for example, the following line would add a reference to the System.Data assembly:

```
<%@ Assembly Name="System.Data.dll" %>
```

After referencing a given assembly, the Import directive allows the developer to access the .NET classes without having to use the fully qualified namespace. The Import directive is the ASP.NET equivalent of the C# "using" keyword (Imports in VB.NET). Note that a given class assembly must first be referenced with the Assembly directive before its namespace is qualified with Import. The following line allows methods inside Global.asax to access the DataReader class (inside the System.Data namespace) without using the fully qualified System.Data.DataReader notation:

```
<%@ Import Namespace="System.Data" %>
```

Object Tag Declarations

Object tags allow the programmer to instantiate session and application objects. The instantiated objects can be either .NET components or any classic COM component. The syntax for declaring a session or application object is as follows:

```
<object id="[someID]" runat="server"
class|progid|classid=Value scope="[objScope]" />
```

The "class" attribute is used to instantiate a .NET component, whereas "progid" and "classid" reference a COM component by ProgID and ClassID, respectively. The "scope" attribute is used to specify whether the object maintains session or application state, as described below.

1. session: Setting scope="session" specifies that each application session (for example, a web browser client) will "own" an instance of the object running on the server. The object lives as long as the session is active. Assume that we have an object with id="myObj" that is an instance of CodeNotes.someClass. This object would be specified in Global.asax as the following:

```
<object id="myObj" runat="server"
  class="CodeNotes.someClass" />
```

The global object myObj can be referenced inside any ASP.NET page in the application via the following syntax:

```
<script language="C#" runat="server">
  someClass obj = (someClass)Session("myObj");
</script>
```

2. application: With scope="application" an instance of the object is shared amongst all sessions of an application throughout its duration. For an ASP.NET page, this can be viewed as a single object shared by multiple web browser instances, possibly on different machines. The following line is used from within any ASP.NET page in the application to access the global object:

```
someClass obj = (someClass)Application("myObj");
```

Remember that session scope is user-specific, while application scope is server-specific. In other words, any object in application scope will have a much longer life span than a session-level object.

Web.config

In ASP, configuration settings for an application (such as session state) are stored in the IIS metabase. There are two major disadvantages with this scheme. First, settings are not stored in a human-readable manner but in a proprietary, binary format. Second, the settings are not easily ported from one host machine to another. (It is difficult to transfer information from an IIS's metabase or Windows Registry to another machine, even if it has the same version of Windows.)

Web.config solves both of the aforementioned issues by storing configuration information as XML. Unlike Registry or metabase entries, XML documents are human-readable and can be modified with any text editor. Second, XML files are far more portable, involving a simple file transfer to switch machines.

Unlike Global.asax, Web.config can reside in any directory, which may or may not be a virtual root. The Web.config settings are then applied to all resources accessed within that directory, as well as its subdirectories. One consequence is that an IIS instance may have many web.config files. Attributes are applied in a hierarchical fashion. In other words, the web.config file at the lowest level directory is used.

Since Web.config is based on XML, it is extensible and flexible for a wide variety of applications. It is important, however, to note that the Web.config file is optional. A default Web.config file, used by all ASP.NET application resources, can be found on the local machine at:

```
\%winroot%\Microsoft.Net\Framework\version\CONFIG\machine.config
```

Note that the directory will vary depending on the version of Microsoft.NET installed.

If you examine machine.config in any text editor, you will observe the following format:

```
<configuration>
<configSections>
<section name="appSettings" type=
  "System.Web.Configuration.NameValueSectionHandler"
/>
<sectionGroup name="system.web">
  <section name="sessionState" type=
 "System.Web.Configuration.SessionStateConfigHandler"
/>
</sectionGroup>
</configSections>

<appSettings>
  ...
</appSettings>
<system.web>
  ...
</system.web>
  ...
</configuration>
```

Listing 8.5   Web.config configuration format

Configuration settings are stored in the Web.config file inside the root <configuration> tag. Let us now examine the various permissible elements under the <configuration> tag.

<configSections>

The <configSections> element is used to define the structure of the Web.config file. Each <section> child declares a section that is permissible in the configuration file, along with the .NET class that processes configuration data in that specific section. For example, Listing 8.5 shows the <section> declaring the appSettings section. Because of this declaration, you will notice an <appSettings> section later on in the Web.config file. This tag is explored in the next section.

It is important to note that the Web.config file does not impose any semantics for a given section, except that all sections must be contained inside the <configuration> root, and each section must be declared in <configSections>. The meaning of data stored in sections such as <appSettings> is left completely to the .NET class that processes the data. The only stipulation for the .NET processing classes is that they must inherit from an interface called /ConfigurationSectionHandler (defined in System.Configuration).

The <configSections> element also allows you to create your own custom sections in the configuration file. We could, for example, create a section called <databases> that would contain the DSNs of all databases used in an application. To do this, we would declare <databases> in the <configSections> area, in the same manner with which <appSettings> is defined. Lastly, we must create a class that inherits from /ConfigurationSectionHandler to process the data in <databases>. This process is described in greater detail at ⊶NET080011.

<appSettings>

The <appSettings> element can be used to store configuration information as value name pairs, which can then be recalled by an ASP.NET page or web service based on a key name. You could for example, embed a Data Source Name (DSN) into the configuration file using the following lines in Web.config:

```
<appSettings>
  <add key="myDSN"
    value="Server=localhost;uid=sa;pwd=;
    database=CodeNotes" />
</appSettings>
```

Listing 8.6   Using the <appSettings> Element

Any ASP.NET resource in the same directory (or subdirectory) as Web.config can reference this key-value pair. For example, the following line shows how to reference the DSN from an ASP.NET page.

```
String dsn = ConfigurationSettings.AppSettings("myDSN");
```

Note that the ConfigurationSettings object is a static object provided by ASP.NET.

<system.web>

If you look in machine.config, you will notice that <system.web> is a container for a variety of configuration sections, including <sessionState> and <authentication>. The <sessionState> element, for example, can be used to configure the specific settings for an HTTP session between a client and the web server. You can use this element to specify whether the client uses cookies to maintain client-side state, or whether the state is stored on a separate machine altogether. For example, the following line in Web.config tells ASP.NET to store session state (for the given web application) on the server, instead of using client-side cookies, and to keep the session valid for 20 minutes:

```
<system.web>
  <sessionState cookieless="true" timeout="20" />
</system.web>
```

Listing 8.7   Applying session state in Web.config

Another child of the <system.web> element is the <authentication> element. The <authentication> allows you to include security features such as HTML Forms Authentication, as well as user/role privileges, to a web application. An article highlighting the specifics of ASP.NET authentication can be obtained at CodeNotes link ᴄᴺ→NET080012.

Examples of these three attributes, in additional to other Web.config attributes, can be found at ᴄᴺ→NET080013.

HOW AND WHY

Can ASP and ASP.NET Applications Share State Variables?

As we discovered in the beginning of this chapter, Internet Information Server (IIS) is capable of housing both ASP and ASP.NET scripts. Because different engines are used to process each script, however, ASP and ASP.NET scripts cannot share state variables.

SUMMARY

The Global.asax and Web.config files are relatively small but highly significant configuration files. First, the Global.asax file provides a common access point for your entire web application. You can use this file to store common code, initialize application and session level variables, and perform all sorts of shared functionality.

Second, the Web.config file replaces both the metabase and Windows Registry configuration hassles from ASP. This single XML file provides powerful configuration features that can be changed and ported between machines quite easily.

Chapter Summary

ASP.NET is an evolution of Microsoft's Active Server Page (ASP) technology. Using ASP.NET, you can rapidly develop highly advanced web applications based on the .NET framework.

ASP.NET offers many significant advantages over ASP and many other server-side web frameworks. Instead of being limited to scripting languages, ASP.NET code can be written in strongly-typed languages such as VB.NET and C#. Code is precompiled and later optimized at runtime by a Just In Time compiler, offering significant performance improvements over ASP.

ASP.NET also features web controls, which are managed classes with events and properties that render themselves as HTML on the client side. These controls are coupled with the Visual Studio Web Form Designer, which allows the design of web applications in an intuitive, graphical method similar to Visual Basic 6. ASP.NET ships with web controls wrapping each of the standard HTML controls, in addition to several controls specific to .NET. One such example is validation controls, which intuitively validate user input without the need for extensive client-side script.

ASP.NET web controls can be bound directly to any data source, from a database to an array. Data-bound controls add a layer of abstraction between data and presentation that simplifies the development of datacentric applications. In addition, web controls such as DataGrid, DataList, and Repeater introduce the idea of templating. With templates, the developer has complete freedom over the appearance of displayed data and is no longer limited to one predefined format.

ASP.NET also offers noteworthy administration improvements over ASP. In ASP, web application configuration is stored in a proprietary metabase format that is difficult to manipulate and transport. In contrast, ASP.NET configuration is stored in XML format, where it can be parsed and easily manipulated.

In many respects, ASP.NET provides major improvements over ASP, and can definitely be considered a viable alternative for rapidly developing web-based applications.

Chapter 9

—

WEB SERVICES

A web service is a software component that exposes itself through the open communication channels of the Internet. Applications running on remote machines, on potentially different platforms, can access these components in a language and platform-independent manner. This chapter presents the facilities .NET offers in creating versatile web services.

To appreciate the advantages of a web service, consider how traditional distributed components are implemented. Most often, distributed components use proprietary distributed architectures such as DCOM, CORBA, or Java RMI to handle request and response messages. While DCOM, CORBA, and RMI are extensive and mature frameworks, they are restrictive in three respects:

1. DCOM, CORBA, and RMI use proprietary object models to communicate between client and server. This means to access a DCOM component, a client must speak COM. Similarly, a basic RMI client can only speak to an RMI server. (RMI and CORBA can crosscommunicate to a certain degree through the Internet Inter-ORB Operating Protocol (IIOP).)
2. Components written with DCOM, CORBA, and RMI communicate over network ports other than 80 (which is used for HTTP). Most corporate IT departments are very strict about opening extra ports on the main firewall, as extra ports increase risk and require greater monitoring efforts.
3. No standardized method exists for publicly advertising DCOM,

CORBA, and RMI components. In this situation, public advertising means that any given client on the Internet has the ability to locate the web service and query its interface for a list of exposed methods, types, and calling conventions.

Web services address the three preceeding limitations by basing their communication mechanism on existing Internet technologies—HTTP and XML. Any client that speaks HTTP and XML can interact with a web service, regardless of language or platform. Also, since HTTP transmits requests over port 80, firewalls are no longer an obstacle.

The third limitation is overcome by two web service technologies: Web Service Discovery (DISCO) and Web Service Description Language (WSDL). DISCO files are XML documents used to advertise the location of web services on the given server. WSDL is also an XML document, but it describes the data types, methods, and calling conventions of a web service. Both of these technologies are discussed in separate sections in this chapter.

Web services must reside on a web server—a dedicated system that ferries incoming HTTP requests to the service and sends any responses back to the client. .NET web services must reside within the Internet Information System (IIS) web server. IIS, in turn, uses the ASP.NET Runtime (Chapter 8) to compile and process the web services, similar to how ASP.NET intervenes with ASP.NET pages.

CORE CONCEPTS

URI

URI stands for Uniform Resource Identifier. URI is a generic term that is used for the addressing of units on the Internet. A Uniform Resource Locator (URL), for example, is a type of URI.

XML Namespace

An XML Namespace is a unique URI that represents a collection of predefined XML elements and attributes. For example, the SOAP namespace ("http://schemas.xml.org/soap/") is used to represent the vocabulary of elements and attributes predefined for the SOAP grammar (e.g., <Envelope>, <Body>, etc.). XML namespaces are generally associated with a prefix, which can then be used to qualify elements and attributes throughout the XML document. XML namespaces are not necessarily existing URIs; they are simply unique strings, recognizable by any application that uses the vocabulary defined within the namespace.

XML Schema

A schema is an XML document that describes the structures, constraints, and relationships of an XML data file. In other words, it prescribes the format of an XML document. As we will see in the WSDL and Web Service Discovery sections of this chapter, both WSDL and DISCO files must adhere to certain schemas.

HTTP

HTTP stands for Hyper Text Transfer Protocol and is the underlying communication protocol behind the Web. HTTP defines how requests and responses between client and server are formatted and transmitted.

The Internet is datacentric—to obtain information, you usually have to provide it. To perform an Internet search, for example, you must provide the subject of the search. This information is transmitted to the search engine, and the search results are returned in a response. In HTTP, this information is communicated as name-value pairs—the name of the variable being sent (in our case it might be SearchSubject) and the contents of the variable. HTTP defines two procedures for querying data over the Internet, namely HTTP GET and HTTP POST. The difference between GET and POST lies in the way the name-value pairs are transported.

An HTTP message consists of two parts, namely the header information and an optional message body. The header information consists of items such as the HTTP protocol to use (GET or POST), the URI of the requested resource, the content-type of the message body, and so on. As we will see in the HTTP POST and SOAP section of this chapter, the format of the message body depends on the protocol used.

HTTP GET

In an HTTP GET request, name-value pairs are transmitted as part of the URI request itself. If you were to perform a search for "CodeNotes" on the popular Google Internet search site, for example, the address on your browser would look similiar to the following:

```
http://www.google.com/search?q=CodeNotes
```

Notice the name-value pair in the URI above. The name of the variable is represented by "q," which possibly stands for query. The value is associated with "q" in our search string, "CodeNotes." HTTP GET requests are formed in the above format, by appending name-value pairs to the URI request, a process commonly referred to as url-encoding.

HTTP POST

Like GET, HTTP POST sends url-encoded name-value pairs to a destination on the Internet. The difference is that name-value pairs are not appended to the destination URI but are embedded in the HTTP request as the message body. When you fill out a customer information form online, POST is often used instead of GET. When using POST, transmitted data is packaged in the message body and does not appear in the URL, affording a greater amount of security.

Either GET or POST can be used to call a web service. GET is often used when the amount of data passed to the component is small and not secretive. POST is desirable in circumstances where the amount of data is large (possibly thousands of bytes) or where security is a concern. We will investigate how a web service uses the HTTP protocol in the following example, as well as the HTTP POST and SOAP and WSDL sections of this chapter.

WEB SERVICE EXAMPLE

In this example we will create a simple Calculator web service that exposes one function—GetRandomNumber(). Web services require that ASP.NET and IIS are installed on the host machine. Both of these products should be installed automatically by the .NET Framework setup.

The first step is to create a directory on your machine that will house your web service (call it C:\MyWebService). The IIS Configuration tool is then used to turn this directory into a virtual directory, which makes files stored in C:\MyWebService accessible to IIS and ASP.NET. Launch the IIS Configuration manager by going to Start Menu → Programs → Administrative Tools → Internet Services Manager. Right-click on Default Web Site. Selecting New → Virtual Directory from the popup menu launches the Virtual Directory Creation Wizard. You will be prompted to give the directory an alias (enter MyService), as well as the actual location of the directory on your machine (enter C:\MyWebService). The creation of the virtual directory is now complete, and all files in C:\MyWebService are available to IIS and ASP.NET via the URI http://localhost/MyService/.

The next step is to implement the actual web service. Using your favorite text editor, create a file in C:\MyWebService called Calculator.asmx. Note that web services are characterized by the .asmx file extension, whereas ASP.NET pages (Chapter 8) have the extension .aspx. As stated at the beginning of this example, our web service will expose one function called getRandomNumber(), which accepts two floating-point parameters x and y, and returns a random floating-point number in-between. Copy the following C# source code into `Calculator.asmx`. A VB.NET equivalent can be obtained at ⇻NET090001.

```
<%@ WebService Language="C#" Class="CodeNotes.Calculator" %>

namespace CodeNotes {
  using System;
  using System.Web;  // Need these two references
  using System.Web.Services;  // for Web Services.

  [WebService(Namespace=
    "http://www.codenotes.com/webservices/")]
  public class Calculator
  {
    [WebMethod(Description=
      "Generates a random number between x and y")]
    public double getRandomNumber(double x, double y)
    {
      Random r = new Random();
      double randDouble = r.NextDouble();
      double returnVal = (y - x) * randDouble + x;
      return returnVal;
    }
  }
}
```

Listing 9.1   Calculator web service (Calculator.asmx)

Notice that the Calculator class in Listing 9.1 follows virtually the same C# syntax that we have used to create other .NET components. Three new syntax features, which are bolded in Listing 9.1, are added to transform the Calculator class into a bona fide web service.

1. <%@ WebService Language="C#" Class="CodeNotes. Calculator" %>. Typically, a web service such as Calculator .asmx remains uncompiled on the server until it is accessed. When a web service is first accessed, it is Just In Time (JIT) compiled by ASP.NET. The <%@ WebService %> descriptor is used to specify the language in which the service is written (C#), as well as the class that is to be exposed (CodeNotes.Calculator). ASP developers will recognize the <% and %> tags used to denote information intended for the web server.

When the Calculator service is first called, ASP.NET will parse the <%@ WebService %> line and invoke the C# compiler (csc.exe) to compile the Calculator class. Alternatively, you do have the option of precompiling your class into an assembly. See the How and Why section at the end of this example for details.

2. [WebService(Namespace="http://www.codenotes.com/web services/")]. The WebService attribute is used to define the XML namespace for a web service. If you are unfamiliar with attributes, please refer to the Attributes section in Chapter 4. As discussed in the Core Concepts section above, XML namespaces uniquely define a collection of predefined XML elements. In this case, the predefined elements are the methods exposed by the web service.

The application of the XML namespace will be examined in more depth in the WSDL section of this chapter. At this point, it is important to note two points about the web service XML namespace. First, the namespace is required to ensure that the GetRandomNumber() method of our Calculator class is unique, as compared to any other Calculator web services on the Internet. Secondly, the specified namespace (in this case http://www.codenotes.com/webservices/) does *not* represent the location of a resource on the Web—the namespace could just as easily have been declared as:

```
[WebService(Namespace="SomeServiceXYZ")]
```

URLs, however, are typically used for XML namespace, since they are inherently unique.

3. [WebMethod(Description="Generates a random number between x and y")]. Every method exposed by a web service must be marked with the [WebMethod] attribute. The [WebMethod] attribute alone transforms the class method into a Web-callable one. The optional Description parameter, on the other hand, allows the developer to provide a human-readable description of the method's functionality. In a later section of this chapter, Other Web Service Features, we will discuss additional [WebMethod] parameters used to manage state and transactions for a web service method.

The [WebMethod], [WebService], and <% WebService %> descriptors transform the C# Calculator class into a Calculator web service. The

remaining lines in Listing 9.1 are straightforward C#. The System
.Random class is used to return a random number within the interval
specified by parameters x and y.

To invoke the web service, launch Internet Explorer and navigate to
http://localhost/ MyService/Calculator.asmx. ASP.NET creates a default
page that depicts the methods exposed by Calculator.asmx, along with a
link called "Service Description." The Service Description is the WSDL
(an XML interface) for this web service and is discussed in detail in the
WSDL section of this chapter. Click on GetRandomNumber() to obtain the
following screen:

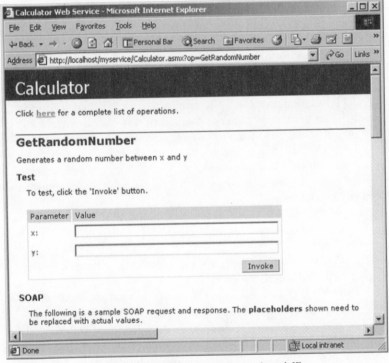

Figure 9.1   Accessing our web service through IE

Note that the Description parameter of the [WebMethod] attribute we
specified in Listing 9.1, "Generates a random number between x and y,"
is parsed by ASP.NET, and appears in Figure 9.1.

Below the description, ASP.NET lists the parameters accepted by the
GetRandomNumber() method, and displays entry fields allowing you to
invoke the method for test purposes. Scroll down the default page, and
note the sections with headings "SOAP", "HTTP POST," and "HTTP

GET." These three sections present example request and response messages in the format required to access the web service. Keep these formats in mind, as we will use this information in the following section, HTTP POST and SOAP.

Test the GetRandomNumber() method by entering values for x and y (say, 0 and 100), and click Invoke. Doing so will bring up a screen with the response from the service. Figure 9.2 shows the output obtained from the GetRandomNumber() method call.

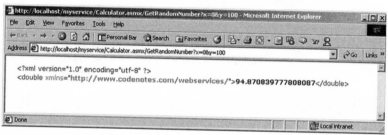

Figure 9.2 GetRandomNumber() results

Notice that GetRandomNumber() returned its result in XML format; this is true for all web service methods. Also note that the XML element containing the random number uses the XML namespace we specified with the [WebService] attribute (Listing 9.1). This namespace distinguishes the result returned by our component from results returned by other web services.

Look closely at the URL in Figure 9.2 and you will see that the x and y values you specified are embedded into the URL itself. From the Core Concepts section of this chapter, you should recognize this format as an HTTP GET request. When the Invoke button (Figure 9.1) was clicked, the following sequence of events occurred:

1. The browser (Internet Explorer, in our case) reads the x and y values from the fields in the HTML page and sends out the following HTTP GET request: http://localhost/myservice/ Calculator.asmx/GetRandomNumber?x=0&y=100
2. IIS and ASP.NET determine that the request is for the Calculator component located in the MyService virtual directory. (Recall that this actually points to the directory C:\MyWebService on the local machine.)
3. If the web service is being requested for the first time, ASP.NET JIT-compiles the component according to the first line in Listing 9.1. Remember the <%@ WebService %> descriptor instructed

ASP.NET to use the C# compiler (csc.exe) to build the Calculator component. After compilation, ASP.NET delivers the following HTTP GET request to the Calculator component:

```
GET /myservice/Calculator.asmx/GetRandomNumber?x=0&y=100
HTTP/1.1
```

Remember that adding the <%@ WebService %>, [WebService] and [WebMethod] tags transformed our C# Calculator class into a web service. One virtue of a web service is that it inherently interprets HTTP requests behind the scenes. The Calculator service determines that a client is calling the GetRandomNumber() method with parameters x=0 and y=100. The Calculator service executes the method to produce a random number between 0 and 100.

4. The Calculator web service packages the result into the XML format of Listing 9.3. This result is returned to the ASP.NET Runtime with the instruction that it be delivered to the client.

5. IIS sends the XML result over HTTP back to the client (in this example, the web browser).

The above steps certainly seem like a roundabout method of obtaining a random number! This scenario is more impressive, however, if you realize that the client could have been anywhere (across the room, across the ocean), and the exposed method could have done anything (queried a database, traded a stock, etc.). Also keep in mind that our client does not have to be a web browser. It can be any application capable of sending HTTP over the Internet. In addition, parameter methods can be transferred using more sophisticated mechanisms such as HTTP POST and SOAP. The next topic will examine these two protocols in detail.

HOW AND WHY

Can My Web Service Class Reside in a Compiled Assembly?
In the previous example we didn't compile Calculator.asmx. Instead, the ASP.NET Runtime JIT-compiled the class when the GetRandomNumber() method was first called. Situations may arise where you want ASP.NET to invoke a web service that is already compiled. One such scenario is when you want to write a web service in managed C++. Unfortunately, ASP.NET can only JIT-compile components written in C#, VB.NET, or JavaScript (by using the Language="C#/VB/JS", options of the WebService attribute, respectively).

To expose a C++ version of the Calculator component as a web service (the source code can be found at ⚓NET090002), compile it into an assembly using the Visual C++ compiler:

```
cl /CLR /LD Calculator.cpp
```

Place the Calculator.DLL assembly file that is produced in the virtual root's bin directory (`C:\MyWebService\bin` in our example). Now create a text file called `CalcCpp.asmx` in `C:\MyWebService` that contains the following line:

```
<%@ WebService Class="CppCalc.CalcClass,Calculator"%>
```

The highlighted portion of the line above tells ASP.NET that the web service resides in the Calculator.DLL assembly (ASP.NET automatically looks in the bin directory for it). Note that when specifying the assembly name, you omit the DLL extension. Also note that we do not specify a `Language`, since ASP.NET will be executing code that is already compiled.

Point your browser to http://localhost/myservice/CalcCpp.asmx and ASP.NET will run the managed C++ class as a web service. This technique can also be used on languages that are not supported by ASP.NET but may produce IL code in the future (COBOL, Java, etc.). You can, if you wish, also use this procedure on classes written in C#, VB.NET, and JavaScript. Because the component is already in an assembly, the initial delay time it takes ASP.NET to JIT-compile it (the first time it is invoked) is eliminated. This is an especially attractive option if target class is large and complex.

SUMMARY

A web service is a component that can be accessed over the Internet. To expose a web service, you must have it run within a web server that feeds it incoming HTTP requests and sends method results back to the client as HTTP responses. In the .NET Framework, web services are housed by Internet Information Server (IIS) and ASP.NET.

A web service resides in an .asmx file, which is JIT-compiled when the web service is accessed, or in a precompiled assembly that is automatically loaded when the web service is invoked. Every method in the web service that is to be made publicly accessible must be marked with the `WebMethod` attribute.

Topic: HTTP POST and SOAP

In this Web Service Example section of this chapter, we used HTTP GET to communicate with the Calculator service. Recall that HTTP GET appends data in name-value pairs to the URI of the web service it is calling. Calling the Calculator's GetRandomNumber() method from the web browser, for example, required the following url-encoded string:

```
http://localhost/myservice/Calculator.asmx/GetRandomNumber?x=0&y=0
```

While simple to use, HTTP GET can be limiting in two situations:

- When you need to pass a lot of information to the web service. If, for example, you need to pass an array of one thousand numbers, each number would have to be appended to the URI. While the HTTP specification does not restrict the length of a URI, many web servers and HTTP clients place practical limits on its length.
- When sensitive information is being transmitted (a credit card number, for example). Appending confidential data to the URI is unacceptable, since it can be easily intercepted and exploited.

In this section we examine two alternative methods of communicating with a web service—HTTP POST and SOAP.

HTTP POST EXAMPLE

When communicating with a web service via HTTP POST, data is embedded as name-value pairs in the HTTP request's message body. Unlike HTTP GET, the name-value pairs do not appear as part of the URI.

In this example we call the Calculator component that we developed in the Web Service Example section of this chapter. Unlike in the Web Service Example, however, we will not use the web browser to communicate via HTTP GET. Instead, we will use a properly formatted HTTP POST request to access the Calculator service. To this end, we employ an HTTP-capable component (Microsoft's MSXML COM Component, version 3.0) from Visual Basic 6.0. The use of VB6 is intentional—it demonstrates that web services can be used outside of .NET with any client capable of sending and receiving HTTP requests. Realize also that our client need not be a Windows component. The client could just as easily reside on a Linux or Macintosh machine.

In Figure 9.1 we showed the default page generated by ASP.NET for the Calculator service's `GetRandomNumber()` method. Revisit this page by launching IE with the following URL:

```
http://localhost/myservice/Calculator.asmx?op=GetRandomNumber
```

Scroll down this page and look under the heading HTTP POST. This section of the page presents the message format required to access the Calculator service via HTTP POST. The request and response messages appear as follows:

```
POST /myservice/Calculator.asmx/GetRandomNumber HTTP/1.1
Host: localhost
Content-Type: application/x-www-form-urlencoded
Content-Length: length


x=string&y=string
```

Listing 9.2   Sample HTTP POST request for the Calculator service

```
HTTP/1.1 200 OK
Content-Type: text/xml; charset=utf-8
Content-Length: length

<?xml version="1.0" encoding="utf-8"?>
<double xmlns="http://www.codenotes.com/webservices/">
  double</double>
```

Listing 9.3   Sample HTTP POST response from the Calculator service

The first four lines of Listing 9.2 are the required headers for the HTTP POST request. Note that /myservice/Calculator.asmx/ GetRandomNumber is the URI of the resource we are requesting—the Calculator service's `GetRandomNumber()` method. The Content-Type specifies the format of the data in the message body. "x-www-form-url-encoded" specifies that data is url-encoded as name-value pairs in the message.

Listing 9.3 describes the format of results returned from the web service. Of particular importance is the line "Content-Type: text/xml". Recall that results from a .NET web service are encoded as XML, regardless of the protocol used to request the service (HTTP GET/POST or SOAP). Note also that the XML result from the service (the <double>

element) is prefixed with the XML namespace we used in Listing 9.1 (http://www.codenotes.com/webservices/). Remember, this does not refer to a resource on the web—it is a namespace that distinguishes the Calculator's `double` result from other web services on the Internet.

Using Listing 9.2 as a template, we now write a Visual Basic application that calls the `GetRandomNumber()` method. You can obtain the full source code online at ^{CN}NET090003, along with compiled binaries for those who do not have access to a Visual Basic compiler. Alternatively, create a new Standard EXE project in VB6. In the Projects menu, select References and add a reference to the Microsoft XML, v3.0 component (WinNT\System32\msxml3.DLL). Add a textbox and one button to your form so that it resembles the interface in Figure 9.3.

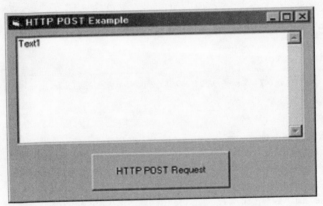

Figure 9.3   Visual Basic HTTP POST application

Double-click on the HTTP POST button and add the code in Listing 9.4 to the button's click event. This code uses the MSXML component to call `GetRandomNumber()`, placing the obtained results in the textbox.

```
'Instantiate the MSXML component
Dim req As New MSXML2.XMLHTTP30

'Specify the URI of our component
'(the second variable specifies synchronous behavior)
req.open "POST",
    "http://localhost/myservice/Calculator.asmx/GetRandomNumber",
    False
'Set HTTP Headers
req.setRequestHeader "Host", "localhost"
```

```
req.setRequestHeader "Content-Type",
  "application/x-www-form-urlencoded"

'Send the HTTP POST request and place results in the textbox
req.send "x=1&y=100"
Dim responseStr As String
responseStr = "Content-Type: " &
  req.getResponseHeader("Content-Type") & vbCrLf
responseStr = responseStr & "Content-Length: " &
  req.getResponseHeader("Content- Length") & vbCrLf
responseStr = responseStr & req.responseText
Text1.Text = responseStr
```

Listing 9.4   Calling GetRandomNumber() using HTTP POST

The req.open line specifies the HTTP Protocol, POST, as well as the URI of the GetRandomNumber() method. The False parameter tells the MSXML component to send the HTTP request synchronously—that is, after calling req.send(), block program execution until a response is received.

The two req.setRequestHeader() calls set the required HTTP headers Host and Content-Type. You might notice that the Content-Length header from Listing 9.2 is omitted. This header (the length in bytes of the HTTP message) is automatically calculated and inserted by the MSXML component.

The req.send() call appends the url-encoded string to the body of the HTTP message and sends the message to the specified HOST. When the HOST responds, the message is displayed in the form's textbox (Figure 9.3). Run the application by pressing F5, click the HTTP POST Request button, and you will see the following response in the textbox:

```
Content-Type: text/xml; charset=utf-8
Content-Length: 120
<?xml version="1.0" encoding="utf-8"?>
<double xmlns="http://www.codenotes.com/webservices/">
  57.845199582560547</double>
```

Listing 9.5   HTTP response message

Listing 9.5 shows that the web service responds to our request with the format described in Listing 9.3.

SOAP OVERVIEW

The third way to communicate with a web service is through SOAP, a frequently acclaimed technology in the .NET Framework. SOAP stands for Simple Object Access Protocol. SOAP prescribes how components communicate with one another using XML messages. Because SOAP uses XML to exchange information, it can more richly describe the data that is exchanged between a client and component (when compared to the HTTP POST and HTTP GET protocols).

At the heart of the SOAP XML message is the SOAP Envelope, which is a container for information being sent to the recipient. As the following listing demonstrates, the Envelope typically defines the XML namespaces used throughout the message.

```
<soap:Envelope
xmlns:soap="http://schemas.xmlsoap.org/soap/envelope/"
 ... >
 --> SOAP Message Contents here
</SOAP-ENV:Envelope>
```

Listing 9.6   *SOAP Envelope*

As Listing 9.6 shows, the SOAP Envelope is defined in the XML namespace http://schemas.xmlsoap.org/soap/envelope/. Also defined in this namespace is the Body element. The SOAP Body specifies the actual operations and data to be processed by the recipient—method calls, for example, along with any required parameters. The SOAP Body element is always a child element of the Envelope, as depicted below:

```
<soap:Envelope
xmlns:soap="http://schemas.xmlsoap.org/soap/envelope/" >
  <soap:Body> ... </soap:Body>
</SOAP-ENV:Envelope>
```

Listing 9.7   *SOAP body*

As its name implies, SOAP is simple. Beyond the predefined elements such as Envelope and Body, SOAP requires only that the contents of the body be a well-formed XML document. SOAP does not prescribe any standard format for calling remote methods, or passing parameters. The interpretation of the data embedded in the Body is left completely up to the recipient of the message, in our case, the web service.

The SOAP specification also defines the elements Header and Fault as children of the SOAP Envelope. The Header element is used to include optional data for the recipient, and is usually used to implement features such as authentication or transaction management. The `Fault` element is a standard method of presenting error information within a SOAP message. While a discussion of the `Header` and `Fault` elements is beyond the scope of this CodeNote, information and examples of their usage can be obtained at ⟲NET090004.

When you call a web service method with HTTP POST, you pass the method parameters in the message body as a url-encoded string. As long as the data type to be transmitted to the service can be broken up into name-value pairs, HTTP POST is sufficient. Consider a web service method that accepts an ADO.NET Dataset as an input parameter (see Datasets in Chapter 6). There is no way to represent this Dataset as a parameter list of name/value pairs. Thus HTTP POST is not sufficient when complex types (nonprimitive) must be transmitted to and from the web service.

SOAP is very similar to HTTP POST, except that the message body is an XML document instead of a url-encoded string. SOAP has an advantage over HTTP GET/POST by virtue of XML's support for representing complex data types. In the XML Support section of Chapter 6, we showed how XML can be used to represent complex heirarchical data structures. Thus, passing a complex structure (such as a Dataset) to a web service requires writing the XML equivalent of the structure and embedding it as the body of the HTTP message.

Although SOAP is more flexible than HTTP GET or POST, there are situations where GET or POST is more appropriate. XML is verbose, and the hierarchical nature of the data requires elements to be nested within opening and closing tags, as depicted below:

```
<someTag>
        <someElement> someValue </someElement>
</someTag>
```

HTTP GET and POST do not support hierarchical data, so you can get away with simply writing:

```
someElement = someValue
```

Compare the HTTP POST and SOAP messages. It is apparent that SOAP messages are significantly longer than their HTTP POST counterparts. When web methods require only primitive data types as parameters, one achieves better performance by using HTTP POST instead of SOAP.

SOAP Example

We will now revisit the default page generated by ASP.NET for the Calculator service's `GetRandomNumber()` method (Figure 9.1). The default page can be viewed at the following URI:

```
http://localhost/myservice/Calculator.asmx?op=GetRandomNumber
```

Scroll down the default page and observe the section entitled SOAP, which displays the SOAP format required to access the Calculator component (recall that this page displays sample HTTP GET, HTTP POST, and SOAP messages). The sample SOAP request message is provided in the following listing:

```
POST /myservice/Calculator.asmx HTTP/1.1
Host: localhost
Content-Type: text/xml; charset=utf-8
Content-Length: length
SOAPAction:
"http://www.codenotes.com/webservices/GetRandomNumber"

<?xml version="1.0" encoding="utf-8"?>
<soap:Envelope
xmlns:xsi="http://www.w3.org/2001/XMLSchema-instance"
xmlns:xsd="http://www.w3.org/2001/XMLSchema"
xmlns:soap="http://schemas.xmlsoap.org/soap/envelope/">
  <soap:Body>
    <GetRandomNumber
xmlns="http://www.codenotes.com/webservices/">
      <x>double</x>
      <y>double</y>
    </GetRandomNumber>
  </soap:Body>
</soap:Envelope>
```

Listing 9.6   Sample SOAP request message

Remember that a SOAP message is an HTTP POST with an XML message body. The first line of Listing 9.6 shows that the POST protocol is being used, and the request URI is the relative path to the Calculator service. Compare this URI with the one used to call the web service with standard HTTP POST (Listing 9.2). Note that when using standard HTTP POST, the URI is of the web service's method, whereas we simply specify the URI of the web service when using SOAP:

```
POST /myservice/Calculator.asmx/GetRandomNumber  (HTTP POST -- Listing 9.2)
POST /myservice/Calculator.asmx                   (SOAP      -- Listing 9.6)
```

The SOAP specification adds the SOAPAction HTTP header to the list of required headers. Note that the SOAPAction header does not point to a valid location on the Internet. Instead, it is the namespace-qualified URI of the requested method.

When calling the service with HTTP POST (Listing 9.2), the Content-Type was set to `application/x-www-form-urlencoded`, since the message body contains a string of name-value pairs. Since the body of a SOAP message is an XML document, we set the Content-Type accordingly to `text/xml` (Listing 9.6).

To call the `GetRandomNumber()` method using SOAP, we need to create an HTTP POST message, set the appropriate headers, and attach a SOAP `Envelope` (formatted according to Listing 9.6) to the message body. Listing 9.6 highlights that SOAP messages are much more verbose than their HTTP POST counterparts. To call the `GetRandomNumber()` method with HTTP POST, we passed the parameters as a name-value string, for example:

```
x=0&y=100
```

With SOAP, we no longer assume that a parameter is a simple type that can be expressed by name and value alone. The `GetRandomNumber()` method is referenced as follows:

```
<GetRandomNumber xmlns="http://www.codenotes.com/webservices/">
    <x> 0 </x>
    <y> 100 </y>
</GetRandomNumber>
```

Note that x or y could just as easily been objects with child XML elements, each with their own data, allowing support for complex types.

To test calling the Calculator web service via SOAP, we will once again use Visual Basic 6 and the Microsoft XML Component, as we did in the HTTP POST example. Source code and compiled binaries for this example can be found at ᴄᴺ⟩NET090005. To create the application yourself, open Visual Basic and create a new Standard EXE. Design a form similar to the following:

Using the code of Listing 9.4 as a template, we once again use the MSXML component to send the SOAP request to the Calculator component. In Visual Basic, double-click on the SOAP Request button (Fig-

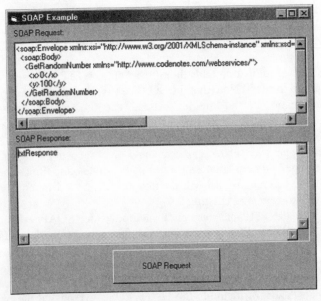

Figure 9.4 SOAP example in Visual Basic

ure 9.4) and add the following code to format the SOAP message according to Listing 9.6.

```
Dim req As New MSXML2.XMLHTTP30
req.open "POST", "/myservice/Calculator.asmx", False

'Set HTTP Headers
req.setRequestHeader "Host", "localhost"
req.setRequestHeader "Content-Type", "text/xml"
req.setRequestHeader "SOAPAction",
"http://www.codenotes.com/webservices/GetRandomNumber"

'Send the SOAP Message.
req.send txtRequest.Text
txtResponse.Text = req.responseText
```

Listing 9.7 Calling the GetRandomNumber() method with SOAP

Note that in Figure 9.4, the top textbox (txtRequest) already contains the SOAP Envelope required to call the Calculator service with parameters x=0 and y=100. Run the application by pressing F5, then click the SOAP Request button. The following information will appear in the bottom text area (txtResponse):

```
?xml version="1.0" encoding="utf-8"?>
<soap:Envelope
xmlns:soap="http://schemas.xmlsoap.org/soap/envelope/"
xmlns:xsi="http://www.w3.org/2001/XMLSchema-instance"
xmlns:xsd="http://www.w3.org/2001/XMLSchema">
  <soap:Body>
    <GetRandomNumberResponse
xmlns="http://www.codenotes.com/webservices/">
    <GetRandomNumberResult>96.088118383701953
    </GetRandomNumberResult>
    </GetRandomNumberResponse>
  </soap:Body>
</soap:Envelope>
```

Listing 9.8   SOAP response message

Compare the response message in Listing 9.8 with the HTTP POST response message in Listing 9.5, and another property of SOAP will become evident: it embeds method results in a SOAP envelope as opposed to the simple XML format used by HTTP GET and HTTP POST.

This example shows that calling a web service with SOAP is a more extensive process than with either HTTP GET or POST. We must first decide on the calling protocol, package and send a properly formatted HTTP request message, and then parse the HTTP response message for the result. Fortunately, the .NET Framework can automate the majority of these operations for us. It can only do this with self-describing information from the component, however, and this is provided by a web service's interface, which is described in WSDL—our next topic.

Given that .NET can abstract these intricate details for us (using proxy classes, which we will examine in the next section), was it necessary to persevere through the preceding example? Remember, you may need to call a web service from a platform where no automation mechanisms exist, in which case you would have to resort to our manual approach (our VB6 example could run on any Win32 environment even without the .NET Framework). In addition, understanding what is occurring behind the scenes is extremely valuable in those esoteric and performance-critical situations where automation may be unacceptable.

WEB SERVICE ALTERNATIVES

Although the web service infrastructure is a convenient way to remotely converse with a component, it does have its disadvantages. Most notably, information is transferred in either key-value pairs or verbose XML over HTTP. Because HTTP is a text-based protocol, if you wish to transfer binary data (an image, for example), it must be converted to a text representation before it can be sent or received. This can severely degrade response time, compounded by the fact that HTTP itself is not a high-performance data protocol.

For performance-critical applications, as well as those that exchange binary data, an alternative worth considering is .NET remoting. Unlike web services, remoting allows you to send data in its native format and also enables you to use faster communication protocols (TCP, for example). By using remoting, however, you forgo the interoperability of web services, as well as the self-describing and discovery mechanisms that we will discuss in the next sections.

For an in-depth discussion of .NET remoting, please see ᴼᴺ▸NET090010, where we discuss the world of remoting, with subtopics such as channels, leasing, activation and singletons.

OTHER WEB SERVICE FEATURES

The .NET Framework exposes several advanced features that enable you to create powerful web services. Some examples are application state, which allows web service components to maintain state between method invocations; transactions, which afford durable protection for those web services that access databases; and security features, which can be used to restrict those users who can access a web service. Information on these advanced topics can be found at ᴼᴺ▸NET090011.

SUMMARY

A web service can accept request messages in one of three protocols: HTTP GET, HTTP POST, and SOAP. The difference between these protocols lies in how information is transferred between the web service and the client. With HTTP GET, information is transferred as name-value pairs, which are appended to the web service's URI: http://.../ GetRandomNumber?x=0&y=100. Although HTTP GET is very simple, appending value-name pairs to a URI can be restrictive when a lot of information needs to be transferred, or when security is a concern.

With HTTP POST, value-name pairs are transferred as part of the HTTP body itself (not appended as part of the URI). This affords a greater amount of security than HTTP GET. SOAP is similar to HTTP POST, except that the HTTP body contains a SOAP XML envelope instead of simple name-value pairs. A SOAP envelope is an XML document that describes the information being transferred to the web service. Because a SOAP envelope is XML, it can transmit complex data types that cannot be described using the simple name-value pairs in HTTP GET and POST.

Topic: WSDL

WSDL stands for Web Service Description Language, and is the way in which a web service describes its interface. WSDL files are XML documents that specify the methods, expected parameters, and types exposed by a web service. WSDL files also contain additional information, such as the transfer protocol (HTTP GET, POST, SOAP) supported by a web service and how invalid method invocations are handled. Those familiar with COM or CORBA can think of WSDL as the web service equivalent of Interface Definition Language (IDL).

WSDL allows client applications to programmatically determine the manner in which a web service is called. In the Web Service Example section at the beginning of this chapter, we examined the default page generated by ASP.NET and used the sample request message to correctly format our HTTP message (refer to Figure 9.1). This process, however, is specific to Microsoft .NET. Remember that web services are simply components accessible on the Internet via HTTP and XML. Given the ubiquitous nature of HTTP and XML, web services can be created in many languages other than C# and VB.NET, and on platforms other than Windows. It is clear that a standard platform- and language-agnostic method of querying a web service's interface is required. WSDL was designed to meet these requirements.

You do not have to manually write WSDL files for web services developed with the .NET Framework; this task is done automatically by ASP.NET. Nevertheless, it is instructive to examine the structure of WSDL for two reasons:

1. You may need to develop a web service for another platform for which automatic WSDL generation is not provided.
2. WSDL exposes the nuts and bolts of a web service, which is useful for debugging. (COM developers can draw analogies to the invaluable OLEVIEW.EXE utility, used to examine a COM component's IDL.)

WSDL is also used by the .NET Framework to generate proxy classes for web services. Proxy classes wrap a web service's interface and hide all of the HTTP plumbing from the developer. Proxy classes allow web services to be used in .NET as any other assembly. The structure of WSDL and proxy generation are demonstrated in the following example.

EXAMPLE

In this example, we will examine the WSDL for the Calculator web service developed in the Web Service Example section at the beginning of this chapter. We will then demonstrate the creation of a proxy class. A proxy class allows us to call the web service from any IL language (C#, VB.NET, managed C++) without having to manually process HTTP request and responses.

To obtain the WSDL for a .NET web service you append "?WSDL" to the web service's URI. Open a web browser and navigate to http://localhost/myservice/Calculator.asmx?WSDL. ASP.NET will automatically generate the WSDL for the Calculator and display the XML document shown in Listing 9.9. Notice the <definitions> element (the parent of the WSDL document), also shown below:

```
<?xml version="1.0" encoding="utf-8" ?>
<definitions xmlns:s="http://www.w3.org/2001/XMLSchema"
  xmlns:http="http://schemas.xmlsoap.org/wsdl/http/"
  xmlns:soap="http://schemas.xmlsoap.org/wsdl/soap/"
  xmlns:soapenc="http://schemas.xmlsoap.org/soap/encoding/"
  xmlns:s0="http:// www.codenotes.com/webservices/"
...
  targetNamespace="http://www.codenotes.com/webservices/"
  xmlns="http://schemas.xmlsoap.org/wsdl/">
```

Listing 9.9   The <definitions> element of the WSDL document

The <definitions> element defines boilerplate XML namespaces used throughout the WSDL document, such as the namespaces for XML Schemas, HTTP, and SOAP. The <definitions> element also includes the XML namespace of the Calculator service (http://www.codenotes .com/webservices/), which we defined in Listing 9.1. Remember, this namespace is essential to distinguish the Calculator service from any other web services on the Internet. Underneath the <definitions> element, you will see the <types> element that describes the methods our web service exposes and the parameters they expect. The <types> element is shown in Listing 9.10.

```
<types>
<s:schema attributeFormDefault="qualified"
  elementFormDefault="qualified"
  targetNamespace="http://www.codenotes.com/webservices/">
  <s:element name="GetRandomNumber">
    <s:complexType>
      <s:sequence>
        <s:element minOccurs="1" maxOccurs="1" name="x"
          type="s:double" />
        <s:element minOccurs="1" maxOccurs="1" name="y"
          type="s:double" />
      </s:sequence>
    </s:complexType>
  </s:element>
  <s:element name="GetRandomNumberResponse">
    <s:complexType>
      <s:sequence>
        <s:element minOccurs="1" maxOccurs="1"
          name="GetRandomNumberResult" type="s:double" />
      </s:sequence>
    </s:complexType>
  </s:element>
  <s:element name="double" type="s:double" />
</s:schema>
</types>
```

Listing 9.10   The <types> element of a WSDL document

As depicted in Listing 9.10, the <types> element contains two other elements, called GetRandomNumber and GetRandomNumberResponse. These elements specify the parameters the GetRandomNumber() method accepts and returns, respectively. Proceed through the rest of the WSDL and you will see the following additional elements:

- <message> elements called GetRandomNumberSoapIn, GetRandom NumberHttpGetIn, etc., which describe how method messages for a certain protocol must be formatted.
- <porttype> and <bindingtype> elements called CalculatorSoap, CalculatorHttpGet, etc., which specify the methods that can be called on a certain protocol.
- A <service> element called Calculator, which specifies the URI the web service can be found at.

It is easy to become overwhelmed by how verbose the WSDL is. Keep in mind that you are inspecting the web service at its most revealing level, which can be incredibly useful during the development process. Examining the WSDL is a powerful way to obtain information that would be otherwise difficult to ascertain (the transfer protocols a web service supports for example). Try adding a new method to the Calculator.asmx file we developed in Listing 9.1, reexamine the component's WSDL, and you will get a better feel for the nuances of WSDL.

Proxy Class Example

We now demonstrate how you can create a proxy class that allows you to call a web service without worrying about the underlying HTTP requests. This requires using a utility in the .NET Framework called WSDL.EXE, which accepts the following parameters:

- /l—specifies the language the proxy class should be generated in. Specify CS, VB, or JS for C#, Visual Basic, or JavaScript, respectively.
- /n—specifies the namespace the proxy class will be contained in.
- /p—determines the transfer protocol the proxy class will use. Allowable values are SOAP, HttpGet, and HttpPost.

Using these parameters we produce a C# proxy class in the CalcProxy namespace for our web service:

```
WSDL /l:CS /n:CalcProxy /p:SOAP
http://localhost/myService/Calculator.asmx?WSDL
```

Notice that after specifying the parameters, we must tell the WSDL.EXE utility where to find the Web Service's WSDL. The utility will produce a file called Calculator.cs containing our proxy class. We now use the C# compiler to produce an assembly that we can call from client applications:

```
csc /t:library Calculator.cs
```

The resulting Calculator.DLL assembly now contains a Calculator proxy class that we can access from a C# program as follows:

```
using System;
using CalcProxy; // reference the namespace the proxy class is in.

public class CallCalc
```

```
{
  static void Main()
  {
    Calculator c = new Calculator();
    Console.Write("Random number between 0-100: ");
    Console.WriteLine("{0}",c.GetRandomNumber(0,100));
  }
}
```

Listing 9.11   CallProxy.cs —calling the Calculator proxy class

Compiling and running this application (csc.exe /r:Calculator.DLL CallProxy.cs) produces the following output:

```
Random number between 0-100: 43.7905868253627
```

Notice that in Listing 9.11 we called the Calculator class like any normal class in the .NET Framework; the proxy took care of the HTTP messages behind the scenes. By using a proxy class, we are completely abstracted from the details of the web service.

HOW AND WHY

What If I Use a Proxy Class That Wraps a Web Service That Cannot Be Accessed?

If you utilize a proxy class that attempts to communicate with an inaccessible web service (if the hosting web server is down, for example), the CLR will generate an error similar to the following:

```
Unhandled Exception: System.Net.WebException: The request
failed with HTTP status 404: Not Found.
```

When using a proxy class, therefore, you must be prepared for the possibility that the underlying web service might be unreachable. This requires that you handle any exceptions that a proxy class might generate. Error-handling example code can be found at ⌖NET090006.

SUMMARY

WSDL stands for Web Service Description Language and is an XML file that describes the methods a web service exposes and the manner in which such methods must be invoked. The most important part of a

WSDL file is the <types> section, which depicts the methods the web service exposes and the parameters they expect. The <message> section of the WSDL file describes how one must package HTTP GET, HTTP POST, and SOAP messages to make requests to the component. Other elements include <porttype> and <bindingtype>, which specify the protocols the web service supports, and the <service> element, which identifies the URI the web service can be found at. You do not manually create WSDL files in the .NET Framework—you generate them automatically by appending "?WSDL" to the URI of the web service itself.

Calling web services in the .NET Framework is greatly aided by a utility called WSDL.EXE. WSDL.EXE will examine a web service's WSDL and produce a web service proxy class. The proxy class exposes all the methods of the web service, and you use it as a generic class in your .NET programs. When you call the proxy class's methods, it packages and sends an appropriate HTTP request to the real web service, and then parses the response that it delivers back to your program. By using proxy classes, you are completely abstracted from the underlying web service protocols.

Topic: Web Service Discovery

In the previous section we learned that a web service advertises its interface using WSDL. By examining a component's WSDL XML file, one can determine the methods exposed by a web service and the manner in which they must be invoked. In order to access the WSDL file, however, we have to know the exact location of the web service. To access the Calculator service's WSDL in the last section, for example, we navigated to the following URI:

```
http://localhost/myservice/Calculator.asmx?WSDL
```

This scenario is acceptable when the location of the service is known ahead of time. Without the exact location, however, there is no way of determining the web services a site exposes (if it exposes any at all). Moreover, one cannot guarantee the language or platform on which the web services or clients run. We need a platform- and language-neutral way to publicly advertise services. This issue is resolved via XML in a process known as web service discovery.

Web service discovery allows others to locate your web services. The location of web services is determined via discovery files, which are

XML documents that itemize the services on a given site. There are two types of discovery files:

1. A static discovery file explicitly lists only those web services you wish to advertise to the outside world.
2. A dynamic discovery file instructs ASP.NET to enumerate and advertise all web services under the URL where the discovery file resides.

One glaring question remains: How does a client know where the discovery document is? How do they discover the discovery file? The convention is to place a link on your website's default page to what is called a global discovery file, which lists all the web services the site exposes (the user must know the location of your website—there is no escaping this requirement). As we will see in the following example, this global discovery file can point to other static and dynamic discovery files on your site. Alternatively, you can make a discovery file itself the default page of your website. Using a discovery file as your site's default page is only feasible, however, if your website is nothing more than a web service storehouse with no user interface. Otherwise clients navigating to your website will be greeted with a verbose XML document.

Note that you are not required to write discovery files. If, for instance, you wanted to keep all of your web services private, discovery files would not be desired. As the following example will demonstrate, however, you can choose which web services are advertised by including only references to them in the discovery file.

The .NET Framework also offers utilities to take advantage of discovery files published by others. A utility called DISCO.EXE interrogates a specified URL and determines if it exposes any web services. The WSDL.EXE utility, examined in the WSDL section of this chapter, creates proxy classes for all the web services listed in a discovery file. Both of these are illustrated in the following example.

EXAMPLE

In this example we will create both static and dynamic discovery files for the Calculator web service used throughout this chapter. We will then show how to employ the DISCO.EXE and WSDL.EXE utilities. The files for this example can be found online at ⊶NET090007.

Static XML discovery files have the .disco extension and begin with the <discovery> element. The <discovery> element can contain two types of child element: <contactRef>, which points to the WSDL for a given web service, and <discoveryRef>, which points to another discovery file. Since our site has only one web service, Calculator.asmx, our static discovery file takes the form in Listing 9.12:

```
<?xml version="1.0" ?>
<disco:discovery xmlns:disco="http://schemas.xmlsoap.org/disco/"
  xmlns:wsdl="http://schemas.xmlsoap.org/disco/wsdl/">
<wsdl:contractRef
  ref="http://localhost/myService/Calculator.asmx?WSDL"/>
</disco:discovery>
```

Listing 9.12   Static discovery file

Notice that we specify the location of the Calculator's WSDL by appending ?WSDL to its URI. To add a reference to a second web service, we would simply add another <contractRef> child to the <discovery> element. Save Listing 9.12 into a file with the .disco extension (i.e., Calculator.disco) and place the file in the virtual root directory for the Calculator service (i.e., C:\MyWebService). This file constitutes a static discovery file that clients can peruse to determine the web services exposed by your site. Clients would examine the <contractRef> element in Listing 9.12, retrieve and examine the WSDL of our Calculator component, and invoke it if desired (you can automate the inspection of discovery files in the .NET Framework using the DISCO.EXE utility, which we will examine shortly).

With static discovery files, we choose which web services we would like to advertise. If our site contained a second web service called Private.asmx, clients would have no way of determining its existence unless we explicitly added it to the Calculator.disco file.

Dynamic discovery files work in the opposite manner. With dynamic discovery, ASP.NET advertises *all* web services under a given URI, unless you explicitly specify which directories to exclude (see the How and Why section on how to do this). Dynamic discovery files begin with the <dynamicDiscovery> element, as shown in the following listing:

```
<?xml version="1.0" encoding="utf-8" ?>
<dynamicDiscovery
  xmlns="urn:schemas-dynamicdiscovery:disco.2000-03-17">
</dynamicDiscovery>
```

Listing 9.13   Dynamic discovery file

Save the contents of Listing 9.13 into a file called myService.vsdisco and place it in the virtual root C:\MyWebService. Note that dynamic discovery files have a .vsdisco extension, whereas static discovery files have a .disco extension. It is also important to note from Listings 9.12 and 9.13 that <discovery> and <dynamicDiscovery> elements are defined in different XML namespaces: <discovery> elements in the DISCO namespace (http://schemas.xml.org/disco/), <dynamicDiscovery> in the namespace "urn:schemas-dynamic-discovery:disco.2000-03-17".

Dynamic discovery lists every web service under a given URI. When the dynamic discovery file is requested, ASP.NET automatically searches the directory containing the discovery file, along with all subdirectories, for any web services. The search results are then returned as a static discovery file. You can test this procedure by opening a web browser and navigating to http://localhost/myService/myService .vsdisco. Your browser will display results similar to the following:

```
<?xml version="1.0" encoding="utf-8"?>
<discovery xmlns="http://schemas.xmlsoap.org/disco/">
<contractRef
  ref="http://localhost/myService/calculator.asmx?wsdl"/>
<discoveryRef
  ref="http://localhost/myService/calculator.disco" />
</discovery>
```

Listing 9.14   ASP.NET-generated static discovery file

The results obtained from ASP.NET correctly locate the WSDL of the Calculator service and report the location of the static discovery file (calculator.disco) that we created earlier in this example. Thus, dynamic discovery not only locates web services, it also detects other discovery files beneath the given URI.

In summary, the static and dynamic discovery files calculator.disco and myService.vsdisco allow clients to determine that our site exposes a Calculator web service. With this knowledge, clients can then obtain the WSDL to determine how to invoke the web service.

DISCO.EXE AND WSDL.EXE

DISCO.EXE is a utility that automates the discovery process. If you point the utility to a discovery file, it will automatically retrieve all the elements to which the discovery file refers. If you execute the following on the command line:

```
DISCO.EXE http://localhost/myService/myService.disco
```

DISCO.EXE will retrieve the following files:

1. calculator.wsdl—the WSDL for our calculator component.
2. myService.disco—the dynamic discovery file we created
3. static.disco—the static discovery file we created

The utility will also create a file called results.discomap, which is an XML report of the files that it retrieved above.

In the WSDL section we saw that we could use the WSDL.EXE utility to create a web service proxy class by pointing it to the WSDL of a component:

```
WSDL /l:CS /n:CalcProxy /p:SOAP
http://localhost/myService/Calculator.asmx?WSDL
```

You can also point this utility to a discovery file, in which case it will create proxy classes for all the web services the discovery file refers to:

```
WSDL /l:CS /n:CalcProxy /p:SOAP
http://localhost/myService/myService.disco
```

HOW AND WHY

How Do I Exclude a Web Service from Being Reported by Dynamic Discovery?

With dynamic discovery, you can only specify exclusion on a per-directory basis. This means that you should move any web services you don't want dynamically reported to a prescribed directory (privateDir, for example). You then stipulate that this directory be excluded from dynamic discovery by using the exclude path element of the discovery file:

```
<?xml version="1.0" ?>
<dynamicDiscovery
   xmlns="urn://schemas-dynamicdiscovery:disco.2000-03-17">
   <exclude path="privateDir" />
</dynamicDiscovery>
```

As a result of this specification, any web service in the privateDir directory will not be reported by dynamic discovery.

Can Dynamic Discovery Handle Nested Virtual Directories?

As its name suggests, a nested virtual directory is a virtual directory within a virtual directory. In the example at the beginning of this chapter, we created a virtual directory called MyService, which really pointed to the local `C:\MyWebService` directory. We could create a nested virtual directory by bringing up the Internet Services Manager, right-clicking MyService, and then selecting New → Virtual Directory. Give the new virtual directory an alias (enter nestedDir), as well as the actual location of another directory on your machine (enter `C:\AnotherDir`). You now have a virtual directory within a virtual directory, and if you point your browser to: http://localhost/myService/nestedDir/someWebService.asmx, IIS will load someWebService.asmx, located in C:\AnotherDir\. The question arises as to whether or not dynamic discovery can detect web services located in nested directories. That is, if you have a dynamic discovery file in the MyService virtual directory (which is really C:\MyWebService), will it detect web services located in the nested virtual directory nestedDir (which is really C:\AnotherDir)?

As of this writing, ASP.NET does not detect web services in nested directories. So, if you point your browser to the dynamic discovery file we developed in Listing 9.13, http://localhost/myService/myService .vsdisco, it will *not* detect any web services in nestedDir. This is thus a second technique (in addition to the `exclude path` mechanism discussed in the previous question) to prevent a web service from being detected by dynamic discovery; by placing an `.asmx` file in a nested virtual directory, it cannot be detected by dynamic discovery files in the virtual root.

SUMMARY

Web service discovery files are XML files that advertise the web services on an Internet site. There are two types of discovery files: static and dynamic. With static discovery files, you must explicitly list all the web services you wish to advertise to the outside world. A static discovery XML file begins with the `<discovery>` element and can contain two types of child elements: `<contractRef>`, which points to the WSDL of a web service, and `<discoveryRef>`, which points to another discovery file. Static discovery files must have a .disco extension.

Dynamic discovery files begin with the `<dynamicDiscovery>` element and instruct ASP.NET to tally all the web services under the URI in which the discovery file resides. After ASP.NET has dynamically determined all of the web services a URI contains, it produces a static discovery file, which can then be inspected by the user. Unlike static discovery files, dynamic ones end with the .vsdisco extension.

By interrogating a discovery file, a user can determine what web services are exposed on your Internet site. Since the discovery file points to a web service's WSDL, a user can scrutinize it to determine where the web service actually resides and the manner in which it must be called.

Chapter Summary

A web service is a component that can be accessed through the HTTP GET, HTTP POST, and SOAP protocols. A web service must be housed by a web server, which conveys incoming requests to the component and then communicates the results back to the client. In .NET, Internet Information Server (IIS) and the ASP.NET Runtime are used to house web services.

A web service resides in a .asmx file, which is JIT-compiled by ASP.NET the first time the web service is invoked. To communicate with a web service, you must send it a properly formatted HTTP GET, HTTP POST, or SOAP message. The major difference between these three protocols lies in how parameters are passed to the web service. With HTTP POST and HTTP GET, parameters are passed as simple name-value pairs (x=0, y=100). With SOAP, parameters are passed using a more complex SOAP XML envelope. The advantage of a SOAP envelope over name-value pairs is that it can describe complex data types such as ADO.NET Datasets, which cannot be communicated using HTTP GET and HTTP POST. The disadvantage of SOAP is that XML envelopes are more verbose than value-name pairs, thus taking more time to transfer and interpret.

A utility in the .NET Framework called WSDL.EXE abstracts users from the details of web service transfer protocols and messages by producing a web service proxy class. The proxy class can be called as a normal class in your .NET programs and takes care of the underlying HTTP response and request messages behind the scenes.

Web services describe themselves to the outside world using WSDL files. These XML files describe the methods a web service exposes, the manner in which they must be called, and additional information about the web service (e.g., the transfer protocols it supports). Another type of XML file, called a discovery file, allows one to advertise all the web services that a given Internet site contains. There are two types of discovery files: static files, which must explicitly list those web services you wish to advertise, and dynamic files, which instruct ASP.NET to automatically advertise all the web services that a given site contains.

Index